Basketball's
Most Wanted

Other Books in the *Most Wanted* Series

Baseball's Most Wanted, by Floyd Conner

Football's Most Wanted, by Floyd Conner

Golf's Most Wanted, by Floyd Conner

NASCAR's Most Wanted, by Jim McLaurin

Soccer's Most Wanted, by John Snyder

Wrestling's Most Wanted, by Floyd Conner

Basketball's Most Wanted

The Top 10 Book of Hoops'
Outrageous Dunkers, Incredible
Buzzer Beaters, and Other
Oddities

Floyd Conner

Brassey's, Inc.

WASHINGTON, D.C.

Library of Congress Cataloging-in-Publication Data

Conner, Floyd, 1951–
    Basketball's most wanted : the top 10 book of hoops' outrageous dunkers, incredible buzzer-beaters, and other oddities / Floyd Conner.– 1st ed.
        p.   cm.
    Includes bibliographical references and index.
    ISBN 1-57488-361-5
    1. Basketball–Miscellanea.   I. Title.

GV885 .C595 2001
796.323–dc21

                                          2001035522

Printed in the Canada on acid-free
paper that meets the American National Standards
Institute Z39-48 Standard.

Brassey's, Inc.
22841 Quicksilver Drive
Dulles, Virginia 20166

Designed by Pen & Palette Unlimited.

First Edition

10 9 8 7 6 5 4 3 2

Contents

Photographs

Introduction

The first basketball game was played at the School for Christian Workers in Springfield, Massachusetts, on December 21, 1891. Basketball was invented by a Canadian named James Naismith and was intended as a form of exercise, not as a competitive game. Originally, there were nine players to a side. Players shot at peach baskets hung from the gymnasium balcony. Because the baskets did not have openings in the bottom, every time a basket was made, someone had to climb a ladder to retrieve the ball. In basketball's first game, this was not a problem—only one basket was scored.

Basketball's Most Wanted recognizes the sport's most memorable players, outrageous characters, and little-known trivia. The book contains top-10 lists of the worst players, most colorful coaches, and craziest plays in college and professional basketball history. The lists feature the unlikeliest heroes, wildest fans, oddest nicknames, buzzer beaters, and the strangest things to occur on a basketball court.

Almost anything can happen in the game of basketball. The gold-medal game of the 1936 Berlin Olympics between the United States and Canada was played on a muddy court during a thunderstorm. An NBA player of the 1940s named

Tony Lavelli entertained fans at halftime by playing the accordion. After Pittsburgh's Helicopter Hentz shattered two glass backboards with thunderous dunks during an ABA game against Carolina, the Cougars' owner sent him a bill to replace them. John Warren of the Cleveland Cavaliers once dunked the ball into the wrong basket. The 1989 North Atlantic tournament was played before empty stands because of a quarantine for a measles epidemic.

Basketball players have had their share of memorable nicknames. Charles Barkley's prodigious appetite earned him the monikers The Leaning Tower of Pizza, The Crisco Kid, Boy Gorge, and The Round Mound of Rebound. North Carolina's George Glamack was nicknamed The Blind Bomber because his eyesight was so poor that he had to look at the lines on the court to determine how hard to shoot the ball. Temple's Bill Mlkvy was known as The Owl Without a Vowel due to his unusual last name. Years before Richard Nixon was called Tricky Dick, it was the nickname of clever guard Dick McGuire.

Many basketball players have gone on to successful political careers. Bill Bradley was an All-American at Princeton and a star with the New York Knicks before becoming a New Jersey senator. Former vice president Al Gore played for the Harvard basketball team. Another presidential candidate, Bob Dole, was a member of the University of Kansas freshman team. Former Florida senator George Smathers was captain of the University of Florida basketball team. Morris Udall, a Democratic presidential candidate, played basketball at the University of Arizona.

Occasionally, basketball can become a contact sport. Boston Celtics' coach Red Auerbach once punched out St. Louis Hawks' owner Ben Kerner prior to a game. NBA official Sid Borgia decked a fan who had been heckling him. Kareem

Abdul-Jabbar broke his hand punching another player. New-berry College's Bobby Bailey set a record for the fastest dis-qualification when he fouled out of a game against Furman in three minutes.

This book introduces you to nearly 700 of basketball's most wanted players. Their offenses and accomplishments range from inept play to game-winning shots, to outrageous behavior. Be on the lookout for these individuals.

The Opening Tip

L et's begin with a list of notable basketball firsts.

1. OLLAMALITZLI

Basketball was not invented until 1891, but another game using a ball and hoop existed previously. Ollamalitzli was played with a rubber ball and a stone ring by the Aztecs in the sixteenth century. A player making a shot was entitled to the clothing of all the spectators. Players on the losing side were less fortunate. Occasionally, the captain of the losing team had his head cut off.

2. JAMES NAISMITH

In 1891, James Naismith, a young Canadian instructor at the School for Christian Workers in Springfield, Massachusetts, was given the assignment of creating an indoor game as a recreational activity for students during the long New England winters.

Earlier, Naismith had designed an exercise in which students threw balls into boxes. He wanted square baskets for

James Naismith, who created the game of basketball in 1891, never envisioned the game as a tough competitive sport. His game, which had substantially different rules than the modern game, was designed as a slow-paced recreational activity that could be played indoors during the long New England winters.

his new game, but the school's janitor, Pop Stebbins, suggested peach baskets, which he nailed to the overhead running track 10 feet above the gymnasium floor. Since there were 18 students in the class, it was decided that there would be nine players on each side. The game consisted of two 15-minute halves. A soccer ball was used in the first contest, and the final score was 1–0. William Chase scored the only basket on a shot from midcourt. Since the peach basket didn't have a hole in the bottom, it was necessary to use a ladder to retrieve the ball after a shot was made. Naismith never envisioned his game as an athletic competition; it was meant as a conditioning exercise. In his lifetime, Naismith played the game only twice. It was suggested that it be called Naismith Ball in his honor, but he preferred the name basketball. Otherwise, the NBA might have stood for Naismith Ball Association.

3. SENDA BERENSON ABBOTT

Senda Berenson Abbott was the director of physical education at Smith, an all-female college in Northampton, Massachusetts. When she learned of Naismith's game, she decided it would make an excellent addition to her curriculum. She stressed its exercise benefits and downplayed its competitive aspects. The first women's collegiate game was played between the freshman and sophomore classes of Smith College in 1893. Male spectators were not permitted to attend for fear they would be titillated by the sight of women in bloomers.

4. SCHOOL FOR CHRISTIAN WORKERS

The first public basketball game was played in March 1892 between the students and teachers at the School for Christian Workers in Springfield, Massachusetts. The students won the game 5–1. Amos Alonzo Stagg, who went on to fame as a football coach, scored the teachers' only goal.

5. BROOKLYN CENTRAL YMCA

The first basketball tournament was played in 1893 in New York City and featured local teams. The tournament was won by a squad from the Brooklyn Central YMCA.

6. TRENTON MASONIC HALL

The first professional basketball game, a contest in which players were paid, may have taken place in 1893 at the Fox Opera House in Herkimer, New York. The first documented professional game was played in 1896 at a Masonic hall in Trenton, New Jersey. Players received $15 each.

7. MINNESOTA STATE SCHOOL OF AGRICULTURE

On February 9, 1895, the Minnesota State School of Agriculture defeated Hamline College of Minnesota 9–3 in the first intercollegiate basketball game. As with Naismith's first game, there were nine players to a side.

8. YALE

The first five-on-five basketball game was played on January 16, 1896. Chicago University, coached by Amos Alonzo Stagg, defeated the Iowa City YMCA 15–12. In March 1897, Yale defeated Penn 32–10 in the first intercollegiate five-on-five basketball game.

9. TRINITY LEAGUE

The first formalized college basketball league was formed in 1900. The Trinity League consisted of three Connecticut schools:

Yale, Trinity College, and Wesleyan. Shortly thereafter, other basketball leagues were formed throughout New England.

10. OSSIE SCHECHTMAN

New York guard Ossie Schechtman owns the distinction of being the first player to score a field goal in a National Basketball Association game. The first game of the Basketball Association of America, which later became the NBA, was played between the New York Knickerbockers and the Toronto Huskies on November 1, 1946. Schechtman made a lay-up in the opening moments of the game to earn his place in professional basketball history. Schechtman played only one season in the league, averaging eight points per game. He finished the season with 162 field goals and a shooting percentage of only 27 percent.

Rules of the Game

B asketball rules have evolved over the years. These 10 rules are no longer a part of the game.

1. NAISMITH RULES

The 13 rules devised by James Naismith formed the basis for basketball. The rules first appeared in *The Triangle,* the newspaper of the School for Christian Workers, on January 15, 1892. Many of the rules are still in use, such as how baskets are scored, the prohibition against running with the ball, and the calling of fouls by an official. However, several of Naismith's rules have also been eliminated over the years. According to Naismith, a basket could be scored by throwing the ball into the basket or by bouncing it into the hoop. A team was awarded a goal if the opposing squad committed three consecutive fouls. A player was disqualified if he committed two fouls and was not permitted to return to the game until the opposition scored a goal. A player could be charged with a foul if he struck another player or if he struck the ball with his fist. If a game ended in a tie, a sudden-death period followed in which the first team to score a goal was declared the winner.

2. CLARA BAER

In the late nineteenth century, when basketball was invented, athletic contests were considered unladylike and inappropriate for women. In 1895, Clara Baer, a teacher at Newcomb College in New Orleans, wrote James Naismith and asked for a copy of his instructions on how to play the game. He responded by sending her a court diagram showing where each player should be positioned. Baer misinterpreted the rules and thought that the players could not leave the areas in which they were stationed. As a result, players were confined to three areas on the court, creating frontcourt and backcourt players. Women also were not allowed to grab the ball from other players. These restrictions hampered the development of the women's game for decades.

3. BASK-O-LITE

Baskets and backboards have come a long way since the peach basket of the first game in 1891. The original baskets were not open at the bottom, so after each goal, the game had to be stopped so someone could climb up and retrieve the ball. Open baskets were not legalized until 1913. The Narragansett Machine Company of Providence, Rhode Island, manufactured a basket which was operated with a pulley and chain. When the chain was pulled, the basket tipped, allowing the ball to drop. Other baskets had chains which could be pulled by the referee to open the bottom. Another invention, the Bask-O-Lite, featured a light bulb which lit up when a basket was made. While a similar device was adopted in hockey to signify goals, the Bask-O-Lite never saw widespread use.

The backboard was not introduced until 1895. The main reason that it was installed was to prevent spectators standing on the elevated running tracks in gymnasiums from inter-fering with the flight of the ball. Early backboards differed greatly in size and shape, and were made of wood or metal. Glass backboards were introduced in 1909 but were briefly banned in 1916 because of a rule requiring white paint on all backboards.

4. **POINT REDUCTIONS**

In 1896 the scoring rules were changed, reducing a field goal from three points to two and the free throw from three points to one.

5. **DRIBBLING**

Originally, the dribble did not exist in basketball. The ball was moved down the court by passing. The dribble was intro-duced by players from Yale University. At first, two-handed dribbling was permitted. In 1904, a rule was instituted which forbade the dribbler from shooting the ball. The rule was not rescinded until 1915.

6. **JACK REYNOLDS**

The rules concerning free throws changed often in the early years of basketball. In 1911, coaching during a game was ruled illegal. The offender was warned on the first violation, and the opposing team was granted free throws for any subse-quent violations. Until 1924, a designated player shot all of his team's free throws. In 1904, Jack Reynolds led the South Philadelphia League in scoring with 78 field goals and 460 free throws. Before 1922, a traveling call or double dribble resulted in free throws being awarded to the opposing team.

7. CAGED ARENAS

During basketball's early years, many courts were surrounded by metal cages designed to keep the ball in play and protect the players from the fans and prevent them from interfering in the game. The caged court was banned in 1929, because the cage blocked the view of the spectators and was dangerous for the players. The term "cagers," referring to basketball players, comes from the days of caged arenas.

8. TEN-SECOND RULE

The 10-second rule was adopted in 1933. Before this rule was put into effect, a player could remain in the backcourt with the ball indefinitely. This led to low-scoring games.

9. JUMP BALLS

One of the most significant rule changes occurred in 1937 when the opposing team was awarded possession of the ball after each basket. Prior to the change, the game was stopped after every basket and a jump ball was called. The clock continued running during the stoppage, reducing the actual playing time by as much as 12 minutes per game.

10. GOAL TENDING

Until 1944, goal tending, the blocking of a shot on its way down, was permitted. Some teams would have a tall defensive player do nothing but stand near the basket to swat away shots. When seven-footers such as Bob Kurland began playing in the 1940s, the goal tending rule was created. Anytime a ball is blocked on its way down, a field goal is awarded to the shooting team.

Acting Up

B asketball movies have ranged from the Hollywood hits *White Men Can't Jump* and *Hoosiers* to the celebrated documentary *Hoop Dreams*. Basketball stars have appeared in movies, and future Hollywood stars have played college and professional basketball. Superstar Michael Jordan co-starred with Bugs Bunny in *Space Jam*. Beau Bridges, who came from an illustrious acting family that included father Lloyd and brother Jeff, played basketball for the UCLA freshman team during the 1960–61 season. After averaging less than a point a game, he wisely concentrated his talents on his acting career. Bridges has appeared in numerous films, including a co-starring role with brother Jeff in *The Fabulous Baker Boys*.

1. CHUCK CONNORS

Chuck Connors starred as Lucas McCain in the popular television western *The Rifleman*. He also starred in *Branded, Arrest, Trail,* and the acclaimed miniseries *Roots*. Before he was an actor, Connors played basketball at Seton Hall and spent three seasons in the National Basketball Association. His best season was 1946–47 when he averaged 4.6 points per game for the Boston Celtics. His most memorable moment came during a pre-game drill with the Celtics when he shattered a glass backboard with a powerful dunk. Connors also played professional baseball with the Brooklyn Dodgers and the Chicago Cubs.

2. ART LINKLETTER

Art Linkletter may seem an unlikely jock, but he was an outstanding basketball player at San Diego State in the early 1930s. He led the Aztecs in scoring for two seasons and finished second in the conference. Linkletter went on to a long and successful career in television as host of *People Are Funny* and *Art Linkletter's House Party*.

3. TOM SELLECK

Tom Selleck was captain of the basketball team at Los Angeles Valley Community College. After transferring to the University of Southern California, he played forward on the Trojans' basketball team in 1966 and 1967. Selleck later starred in the long-running television series *Magnum, P.I.* and films such as *Her Alibi* and *Three Men and a Baby*.

4. MIKE WARREN

Mike Warren was a starting guard for two national championship teams at UCLA. As a sophomore in 1966, he averaged 16.6 points per game for the Bruins. Warren was selected to the National Collegiate Athletic Association (NCAA) all-tournament team in 1967 and 1968. He was drafted by the Seattle Supersonics but did not play in the NBA. As an actor, he is best known for his role as officer Bobby Hill in the award-winning police series *Hill Street Blues*.

5. **TED CASSIDY**

Actor Ted Cassidy played the solemn butler Lurch on the sit-com *The Addams Family*. He also played a member of the Hole-in-the-Wall gang in the movie *Butch Cassidy and the Sundance Kid*. The 6'9" Cassidy played basketball at Stetson College and averaged 17.7 points and 10.7 rebounds as a senior in 1955.

6. **KAREEM ABDUL-JABBAR**

Few, if any, basketball players can match the accomplishments of Kareem Abdul-Jabbar. As Lew Alcindor, he led UCLA to three national championships from 1967 to 1969 and was twice voted national collegiate player of the year. A 19-time All-Star and six-time MVP, he holds the record for most points scored in NBA history.

His most notable film role was as a pilot in the hilarious comedy *Airplane!* He also appeared with fellow superstar Julius Erving in *The Fish That Saved Pittsburgh*, a comedy about a basketball team that uses astrology to win games.

7. **ALLAN HOUSTON**

Allan Houston averaged 21.9 points per game in four seasons with the University of Tennessee. The guard scored nearly 20 points a game for the New York Knicks during the 1999–00 season. In 2000, he co-starred with Claudia Schiffer in the film *Black and White*.

8. **HANK LUISETTI**

Hank Luisetti revolutionized basketball with his one-handed shot. Prior to his popularizing the shot, players heaved the

Lew Alcindor (later Kareem Abdul-Jabbar) was the most dominant college player of all time. Largely because of him, the University of California–Los Angeles (UCLA) was almost unbeatable during the late 1960s. His brilliant play continued in the NBA, where he holds the record for most career points.

ball toward the basket with two hands. The Stanford All-American was a prolific scorer and made headlines with a 50-point outburst against Duquesne University on New Year's Day, 1938. That same year Luisetti co-starred with Betty Grable in the forgettable film *Campus Confessions.* The movie did not lead to an acting career, but it did result in him losing his amateur status for a year.

9. **MIKE CONNORS**

Mike Connors's long acting career was highlighted by his title role in the popular private-eye series *Mannix,* which aired from 1967 to 1975. He averaged 9.6 points per game for the UCLA freshman basketball team during the 1946–47 season.

10. **JIM LUISI**

Jim Luisi played one year with the NBA's Baltimore Bullets, averaging 2.9 points per game during the 1953–54 season. His acting credits include his role as Lt. Chapman in the television series *The Rockford Files.*

Playing Politics

M any players have excelled in both a basketball arena and the political arena. Jay Dickey scored eight points per game for the University of Arkansas during the 1959–60 season. He later served as a congressman representing Arkansas' Fourth District. Lee Hamilton led DePauw University (Indiana) in scoring as a junior in 1951 and later was elected to the United States House of Representatives from Indiana's Ninth District. Joe Teasdale was a starter on the 1954 St. Benedict's College (Kansas) team that won the National Association of Intercollegiate Athletes tournament. Teasdale served as governor of Missouri from 1977 to 1981. Larry O'Brien, who was named NBA commissioner in 1975, was chairman of the Democratic National Committee when the Watergate burglars broke into his office in 1972.

1. **BILL BRADLEY**

Bill Bradley averaged more than 30 points a game during his three seasons at Princeton from 1963 to 1965. He led the Tigers to a Final Four appearance in 1965 and scored 58 points in the consolation game against Wichita State. Bradley was named national player of the year in 1965. He played 10 seasons with the New York Knicks and started on their NBA championship teams in 1970 and 1973. He was elected to the Basketball Hall of Fame in 1982. The Rhodes Scholar was elected to the United States Senate representing the state of New Jersey and made an unsuccessful run for the 2000 Democratic presidential nomination.

2. **AL GORE**

Al Gore scored nearly three points per game as a member of the 1966 Harvard freshman basketball team. Upon graduation, he began a distinguished political career, representing Tennessee in the Senate and serving two terms as vice president during the Clinton administration. He was narrowly defeated in the 2000 presidential election.

3. **BOB DOLE**

Bob Dole played for the Kansas freshman basketball team in 1942 before enlisting in the army during World War II. Elected to the United States Senate in 1969, he served as majority leader from 1985 to 1987. In 1976, he was the Republican nominee for vice president on the Gerald Ford ticket. Twenty years later, Dole was the Republican candidate for president but was defeated by Bill Clinton.

4. **MO UDALL**

Mo Udall led the University of Arizona in scoring with a 13.3 average during the 1947–48 season. Voted All-League, he finished second in the conference in scoring. Before entering politics, Udall played a season of professional basketball with the Denver Nuggets of the National Basketball League. Udall served several terms in the House of Representatives and made an unsuccessful run for the Democratic presidential nomination.

5. **RAYMOND FLYNN**

Raymond Flynn averaged nearly 19 points a game for Providence College during the 1962–63 season. The guard played on the National Invitational Tournament championship teams of 1961 and 1963 and was voted MVP of the tournament as a senior. Flynn later was elected mayor of Boston.

6. **EDDIE DURNO**

Eddie Durno led the Pacific Coast Conference in scoring while playing for the University of Oregon during the 1918–19 season. In 1961, he was elected to the United States House of Representatives.

7. **HANK NOWAK**

Hank Nowak averaged more than 20 points a game as a senior at Canisius College and became the school's all-time leading rebounder. Beginning in 1975, Nowak served nine terms as a congressman from the state of New York.

8. **SCOTTY BAESLER**

Before entering politics, Scotty Baesler played guard for the University of Kentucky from 1960 to 1963. He averaged more than eight points a game during his varsity career. Baesler served 10 years as mayor of Lexington, Kentucky, beginning in 1982, and was elected to the United States House representing Kentucky's Sixth District.

9. GEORGE SMATHERS

A close friend of President John F. Kennedy, George Smathers served as senator from Florida from 1950 to 1969. He was captain of the University of Florida basketball team in 1936.

10. TONY MASIELLO

Tony Masiello averaged nearly 20 points per game while playing for Canisius in 1969. Years later, Masiello was elected mayor of Buffalo, New York.

Touching All Bases

Sandy Koufax attended the University of Cincinnati on a combination baseball-basketball scholarship. The Hall of Fame pitcher averaged 9.7 points per game on the Bearcat freshman team in 1954. Steve Hamilton was the only athlete to play in both the NBA finals and the World Series. He was a member of the Minneapolis Lakers in 1959 and pitched for the pennant-winning New York Yankees in 1963 and 1964. Before belting 382 home runs in the major leagues, Frank Howard averaged more than 20 points and 15 rebounds for Ohio State in 1957. Lou Boudreau, Walt Dropo, Robin Roberts, Sonny Siebert, Kenny Lofton, and Dave Winfield were all college basketball stars who went on to become outstanding major-league players.

1. DICK GROAT

Dick Groat was an All-American guard at Duke. His 26.0 scoring average in 1952 was second in the nation, and he once scored 48 points in a game against North Carolina. He was named the Helms Foundation Player of the Year. At the time he left Duke, Groat held the record for points in a career. He averaged nearly 12 points per game for the Fort Wayne Pistons of the NBA in 1953. Groat gave up his basketball career to concentrate on baseball. An outstanding shortstop, he won the batting title and was voted the National League MVP in 1960. He played on world-champion teams with the Pittsburgh Pirates in 1960 and with the St. Louis Cardinals in 1964. He retired in 1967 with 2,138 hits.

2. DAVE DEBUSSCHERE

A promising pitcher with the Chicago White Sox, Dave DeBusschere compiled a 2.90 earned run average during his two-year major-league career. DeBusschere averaged 26.8 points as a senior at the University of Detroit in 1962. He spent 12 seasons in the NBA with the Detroit Pistons and New York Knicks, averaging 16.1 points and playing on two championship teams in New York.

3. RON REED

Ron Reed averaged 20 points and 17 rebounds during his junior season at Notre Dame. He played two seasons with the Detroit Pistons and averaged 8.5 points in 1967. He won 146 games during his 19-year major-league career. His best season came in 1969 when he won 18 games.

4. BOB GIBSON

Bob Gibson averaged more than 20 points a game with Creighton University and then played for the Harlem Globetrotters from 1957 to 1958. Gibson was even better at baseball. A five-time 20-game winner, Gibson notched 251 victories for the St. Louis Cardinals from 1959 to 1975. In 1968, he had one of the greatest seasons in major-league history. Gibson won 22 games, pitched 13 shutouts, and recorded an incredible 1.12 earned run average, the lowest of the modern era. In three World Series, Gibson compiled a 7-2 record with a 1.89 earned run average. He set a World Series record when he struck out 17 Detroit Tigers during a 1968 game. Bob Gibson was elected to the Baseball Hall of Fame in 1981.

5. GENE CONLEY

Gene Conley was one of the few athletes who was able to maintain successful careers in basketball and baseball simultaneously. He pitched in the major leagues from 1952 to 1963, winning 91 games for the Braves, Phillies, and Red Sox. He played on pennant-winning teams in Milwaukee in 1957 and 1958. His best season was in 1954 when he compiled a 14-9 record and a 2.96 earned run average for the Milwaukee Braves. The 6'8" Conley played six seasons in the NBA. His best season was 1963 when he averaged nine points per game for the New York Knicks. He played on championship teams with the Boston Celtics in 1959, 1960, and 1961.

6. JOE GIBBON

Joe Gibbon of the University of Mississippi finished second in the NCAA in scoring during the 1956–57 season. His 30-point average placed him ahead of such stars as Seattle's Elgin Baylor and Kansas' Wilt Chamberlain. Gibbon pitched in the major leagues from 1960 to 1972 for Pittsburgh, San Francisco, Cincinnati, and Houston. The left-hander won 61 games and appeared in the World Series for the Pittsburgh Pirates in 1960.

7. JACKIE ROBINSON

Before he broke baseball's color barrier in 1947, Jackie Robinson was a basketball star at UCLA. He led the Pacific Coast Conference in scoring in 1940 and 1941. Robinson played baseball for the Brooklyn Dodgers for 10 seasons. In 1949 he won the National League batting title with a .342 average. He retired in 1956 with a .311 career average. In 1999, he was selected as the greatest second basemen in baseball history in a nationwide poll of fans.

8. DANNY AINGE

Danny Ainge played for the Toronto Blue Jays from 1979 to 1981. The versatile Ainge saw time at second base, shortstop, third base, and in the outfield, but his career batting average was a disappointing .220. Ainge was an All-American basketball player at Brigham Young. An outstanding guard, he played for more than a decade in the NBA and was a member of championship teams with the Boston Celtics in 1984 and 1986.

9. DON KESSINGER

Don Kessinger scored 23.5 points per game during his senior season at the University of Mississippi. On February 2, 1963, he scored 49 points versus Tulane. Ten days later, he once again rippled the nets in a 48-point performance against Tennessee. Kessinger played shortstop in the major leagues from 1964 to 1979. A six-time All-Star, he played for the Chicago Cubs, St. Louis Cardinals, and Chicago White Sox.

10. **JOE ADCOCK**

An outstanding basketball player, Joe Adcock averaged 18.6 points a game for Louisiana State University during the 1945–46 season. Adcock played first base and outfield for the Cincinnati Reds, Milwaukee Braves, Cleveland Indians, and California Angels from 1950 to 1966. The power hitter belted 336 home runs and played in two World Series with Milwaukee. On July 31, 1954, in a game against the Brooklyn Dodgers, the Braves' first baseman smashed four home runs and a double, setting a major-league record with 18 total bases.

Field Goals

A few players have been able to excel in both basketball and football. Rick Casares led the University of Florida basketball team in scoring and rebounding in 1952 and 1953. In 1957, he led the National Football League in rushing as a member of the Chicago Bears and scored 60 touchdowns during his 12-year pro football career. Ray Evans of the University of Kansas was elected to the College Football Hall of Fame as well as being named to the All-American basketball team in 1942 and 1943. Paul Tagliabue, the commissioner of the NFL, averaged more than 11 points per game during his college basketball career at Georgetown. R. C. Owens caught 206 passes during an NFL career that lasted from 1957 to 1964. A basketball star at the College of Idaho, he averaged 23.5 points and 27.1 rebounds, outrebounding teammate Elgin Baylor.

1. CHARLIE WARD

Charlie Ward won the 1993 Heisman Trophy in recognition of his outstanding play as quarterback for Florida State. A two-sport star, Ward became a point guard for the NBA's New York Knicks.

2. BUD GRANT

A basketball star at the University of Minnesota, Bud Grant played two seasons in the NBA with the Minneapolis Lakers and was a member of their 1950 championship team. He also played two seasons as an end with the NFL Philadelphia Eagles. In 1952, he caught 56 passes and scored seven touchdowns for the Eagles. He led the Canadian Football League in receptions in 1953, 1954, and 1956 while playing for the Winnipeg Jets. He later coached Winnipeg to four CFL championships. As head coach of Minnesota from 1967 to 1985, Grant led the Vikings to four Super Bowl appearances and was elected to the Pro Football Hall of Fame.

3. OTTO GRAHAM

Playing basketball for Northwestern, Otto Graham finished second in the Big Ten in scoring as a sophomore and junior. Graham played professional basketball for the Rochester Royals of the National Basketball League and was a member of the 1946 championship team. Enshrined in both the college and pro football halls of fame, Graham was one of the game's greatest quarterbacks. He played for the Cleveland Browns from 1946 to 1955 and led his team to the league championship game all 10 seasons.

4. JIM BROWN

Jim Brown averaged nearly 15 points per game as a sophomore with the Syracuse University basketball team. An All-American running back, Brown once scored 43 points in a game against Colgate University. He played for the Cleveland Browns from 1957 to 1965 and led the NFL in rushing eight times in nine seasons. Brown, often called the greatest professional football player of all time, scored 126 touchdowns.

5. TERRY BAKER

Oregon State quarterback Terry Baker led the nation in total offense in 1962 and was awarded the Heisman Trophy, which recognizes the best player in college football. In 1963, Baker was the second leading scorer on the school's basketball team, which reached the Final Four.

6. DIKE EDDLEMAN

On the gridiron, Dwight "Dike" Eddleman set numerous records at the University of Illinois, including school records for the longest punt (88 yards) and longest punt return (92 yards). An All-American in basketball, he led the Fighting Illini in scoring in 1948 and 1949. Eddleman played four seasons in the NBA. The forward averaged 15.3 points per game for the Tri-Cities Blackhawks in 1951.

7. WARREN AMLING

College football Hall-of-Famer Warren Amling was an All-American lineman with Ohio State in 1945 and 1946. Amling was also a starting guard for the Buckeye basketball teams that reached the Final Four in 1945 and 1946.

8. CHUCK CARNEY

Chuck Carney was an All-American end at the University of Illinois in 1920. Also an All-American in basketball, Carney led the Big Ten in scoring in 1920 and 1922. He was named national player of the year for the 1921–22 season.

9. **RON WIDBY**

Ron Widby averaged 22.1 points per game for the University of Tennessee in 1967. Named conference player of the year, Widby scored 50 points in a game against Louisiana State University. He played one season with New Orleans of the ABA. Widby was a punter for the Dallas Cowboys and Green Bay Packers from 1968 to 1973 and played for the Cowboys in Super Bowl V.

10. **CORNELL GREEN**

Cornell Green averaged 25.6 points for Utah State during the 1961–62 season. He completed his college career as Utah State's all-time leading scorer and rebounder. He was a star defensive back for the Dallas Cowboys from 1962 to 1974. A five-time Pro Bowl selection, he intercepted 34 passes during his career.

The Sporting Life

These basketball players were even more talented in other sports.

1. TONY TRABERT

Tony Trabert averaged nearly seven points per game for the University of Cincinnati basketball team in 1951. That same year, he won the NCAA singles title in tennis. Trabert went on to win the French Open, Wimbledon, and the United States Open singles crown in 1955. He was elected to the International Tennis Hall of Fame.

2. JACKIE JOYNER-KERSEE

Jackie Joyner-Kersee averaged 9.6 points per game during her basketball career at UCLA. A track and field legend, she won Olympic gold medals in the heptathlon in 1988 and 1992 and the long jump in 1988.

3. JIM BAUSCH

Jim Bausch was a starter for the Kansas basketball team during the 1929–30 season. In 1932, Bausch won the gold medal in the decathlon at the Los Angeles Olympic games.

The following year, he played tailback, defensive back, and linebacker for Chicago and Cincinnati of the NFL.

4. RAFER JOHNSON

Rafer Johnson averaged 8.2 points as a member of the UCLA basketball team in 1959. At the 1960 Rome Olympics, Johnson won the gold medal in the decathlon.

5. HARLOW ROTHERT

Harlow Rothert was an All-American guard at Stanford in 1929. Rothert also won the silver medal in the shot put at the 1932 Summer Olympics.

6. JOE CAMPBELL

Despite standing only 5′7″, Joe Campbell averaged almost 12 points a game for Purdue during the 1956–57 season. The NCAA golf champion of 1955, Campbell won three tournaments on the PGA Tour between 1961 and 1966.

7. SAMMY URZETTA

Sammy Urzetta led the nation in free-throw percentage in 1948 and 1950 while playing guard for St. Bonaventure. In 1950, Urzetta won the United States Amateur Golf Championship.

8. WALTER DAVIS

Walter Davis averaged more than 15 points per game as a senior on the Texas A & M basketball team. From 1953 to 1958, he played professional basketball for the Philadelphia Warriors and St. Louis Hawks. A world record holder in the high jump, Davis won the gold medal at the 1952 Olympics.

9. **RANDY MATSON**

Powerful Randy Matson averaged eight points and 10 rebounds for the Texas A & M basketball team during the 1965–66 season. In 1965, Matson became the first athlete to throw a shot put more than 70 feet. Two years later he won the Sullivan Award, given to the nation's outstanding amateur athlete. Matson also won the gold medal for the shot put at the 1968 Mexico City Olympics.

10. **JOHN RAMBO**

John Rambo averaged more than 20 points and 12 rebounds for Long Beach State during the 1964–65 season. Rambo was the bronze-medal winner in the high jump at the 1964 Olympics.

Olympic Moments

The United States has dominated Olympic men's basketball. Here are some of the Olympics' most memorable basketball games.

1. 1972 GOLD-MEDAL GAME

The United States had never lost an Olympic basketball game heading into the gold-medal matchup against the Soviet Union at the 1972 Olympic games. The U.S. team had amassed a 62-game winning streak on its way to seven consecutive gold medals. The Soviets led by eight points with six minutes to play when the Americans mounted a comeback. With three seconds remaining, Doug Collins made two free throws to give the Americans their first lead of the game, 50–49. It appeared that the United States had once again won the gold medal when the Soviets inbounded the ball and were unable to score before time ran out.

But the Soviet coach, Vladimir Kondrashkin, claimed he had called a time-out. In the confusion, William Jones, the secretary-general of the International Basketball Association, instructed the officials to reset the clock to three seconds, although he had no authority to do so. Given another chance, Ivan Yedeshsko threw a length-of-the-court pass to Sasha Belov, who made a lay-up at the buzzer to give the Soviet Union a stunning 51–50 victory. The Americans protested the game, but the Jury of Appeal ruled 3–2 in favor of letting the result stand. The American team then protested the ruling by refusing to accept their silver medals.

2. 1936 OLYMPIC GOLD-MEDAL GAME

The first Olympic basketball tournament took place in 1936 in Berlin. The games were played outdoors on tennis courts made of clay and sand. On the day of the gold-medal game between the United States and Canada, the court was turned to mud by a downpour. It was nearly impossible to dribble, and the players struggled to shoot the wet basketball. The United States won the game 19–8.

3. INTERNATIONAL BASKETBALL FEDERATION

At the beginning of the 1936 Olympic basketball tournament, the International Basketball Federation inexplicably passed a rule banning all players taller than 6′3″. The United States, which would have lost three players to the ruling, filed a protest, and the rule was withdrawn.

4. BOB KURLAND

The United States easily won the gold medal at the 1948 London Olympics. Led by seven-foot center Bob Kurland, the Americans' average winning margin was more than 33 points per game. In a game against China, one of the Chinese players dribbled between the legs of the towering Kurland and made a lay-up.

5. **IRAQ**

The 1948 Iraq basketball team may have been the worst in Olympic history. They lost by more than 100 points to Korea and China, two teams with losing records. Iraq's average losing margin for the tournament was an astounding 81 points.

6. **WORLD'S COLLEGE BASKETBALL CHAMPIONSHIP**

Although basketball did not become an Olympic sport until 1936, it was featured as an exhibition sport at the 1904 Olympics in St. Louis. The tournament, which was called the Olympic World's College Basketball Championship, featured three American teams, Hiram College, Latter Day Saints' College, and Wheaton College. Hiram defeated Wheaton 25–20 and the Latter Day Saints' College (now known as Brigham Young University) 25–18 to win the title.

7. **1952 OLYMPIC GOLD-MEDAL GAME**

The 1952 gold-medal game at Melbourne featured teams from the United States and the Soviet Union. The outmatched Soviets tried to slow the game in order to keep the score close. Late in the second half, nursing a six-point lead, the Americans began their own stall. One Soviet player sat on the court in disgust. Despite shooting only 20 percent from the field, the Americans prevailed 36–25.

8. **URUGUAY**

Opposing players and officials discovered at the 1952 Olympics that playing Uruguay could be hazardous to their health. Late in a game against France, Uruguay was forced to play with only three players because the rest of the team had fouled out. When France won the game on a last-second basket, Uruguayan players and spectators savagely attacked American referee Vincent Farrell. He was repeatedly kicked in the groin and had to be carried off the court. Two players from Uruguay were banned from the Olympics for their participation in the assault. In a game against the Soviet Union, three Russian players were injured by the foul-prone Uruguayans. The violence culminated in the bronze-medal game against Argentina. The game was marred by an on-court melee that involved more than two dozen players and fans. Despite finishing with only four players, Uruguay won the game and the bronze medal.

9. 1988 SEMIFINAL GAME

Going into the 1988 Olympic Games, the United States basketball team had been defeated only once, the controversial loss to the Soviet Union in the 1972 gold-medal game. There was no disputing the result when the Soviet Union beat the Americans 82–76 in the semifinal game of the 1988 Olympics.

10. RAMUNAS SISKAUSKAS

After its defeat at the 1988 Olympics, the United States decided to replace its team of college players with a team of mostly NBA stars. The so-called "Dream Team" easily won the Olympic gold medals in 1992 and 1996. However, the 2000 American team appeared on its way to defeat against Lithuania when Ramunas Siskauskas was fouled with 43 seconds left in the game. Siskauskas had not missed a free throw in the Olympic tournament. If he converted, he would have given his team a three-point lead. Incredibly, he missed two of the three free throws, and the United States rallied for an 85–83 victory. The Americans went on to win the gold medal, but the Dream Team's air of invincibility was shattered.

Money Shots

Professional basketball players are among the most highly paid athletes. Shaquille O'Neal, the superstar center of the Los Angeles Lakers, signed a 10-year contract valued at more than $208 million. Playing basketball has not always been so profitable.

1. ABE SAPERSTEIN

The Harlem Globetrotters were founded in 1927 by Abe Saperstein. The touring African-American team has entertained millions over the years with its skill and comic routines. In the early days, Saperstein discovered a unique way of rewarding his players for performing a comic bit. Rather than give them a bonus, he took them out of the game for a rest.

2. FRED COOPER

The first professional basketball game was played at a Masonic hall in Trenton, New Jersey, in 1896. The players, with one exception, were paid $15 each. Fred Cooper, captain of the winning team, was given a one-dollar bonus, raising his take for the game to $16.

3. GEORGE GERVIN

George Gervin was one of the greatest scorers in professional basketball history, posting 26,595 points and winning four scoring titles during a pro career that lasted from 1972 to 1986. Despite his great talent, he almost lost his opportunity to play professional ball. He was expelled from Eastern Michigan University for punching an opposing player. For a time, Gervin was paid $40 a game to play for the Pontiac Chapparrals, a minor-league team. His play was so outstanding that he was signed by the Virginia Squires of the ABA in 1972. In 1976, Gervin made his NBA debut with the San Antonio Spurs.

4. CAVEMAN BARLOW

Tom Barlow was nicknamed "Caveman" because of his Neanderthal behavior on the court. His rough play helped the Philadelphia Warriors win the 1926 world title over the Boston Celtics. Barlow was paid $45 per game, making him the highest-paid professional basketball player of his time.

5. STANFORD

The NCAA tournament has become a multi-million-dollar sporting event, but this was not the case in the early years. When Stanford won the 1942 NCAA title, the team received nothing but a check for $93.75 to cover its expenses in Kansas City.

6. POP GATES

William "Pop" Gates was an African-American star who signed with the New York Rens in 1938. Gates led the Rens to a 111-22 record and victory in the World Professional Championship. The rookie sensation was signed to a contract for $125 per month.

7. NEW ENGLAND LEAGUES

In 1898, the first professional leagues were formed in New England. Players received salaries that ranged from $150 to $225 per month.

8. WILT CHAMBERLAIN

Wilt Chamberlain made basketball history on March 2, 1962, when he scored a record 100 points as his Philadelphia Warriors defeated the New York Knicks 169–147. In April 2000, a ball used in the game sold for $551,844, even though there was some doubt of its authenticity. At the time he set the record, Chamberlain was making less than $100,000.

9. BILL RUSSELL

In 1965, Wilt Chamberlain signed a contract for the then impressive sum of $100,000 per year. Although Chamberlain had set numerous scoring records, including averaging more than 50 points a game during the 1961–62 season, he had not yet led his team to an NBA title.

Bill Russell, however, was in the midst of a career in which he led the Boston Celtics to 11 NBA championships in a 13-year span. The five-time MVP was insulted when the Celtics offered him a contract for $70,000. He insisted that he be paid $100,001, one dollar more than his rival, Chamberlain.

10. MICHAEL JORDAN

The explosion in popularity of the NBA during the 1990s resulted in escalating salaries. Michael Jordan was paid $33.14 million by the Chicago Bulls for the 1997–98 season. A Fleer rookie card of Michael Jordan in gem-mint condition was valued at $32,000.

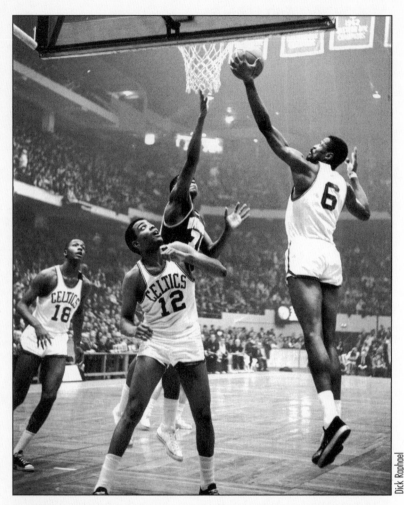

Dick Raphael

Hall-of-Famer Bill Russell, *right,* grabs another rebound at the Boston Garden. Russell's fierce competitiveness and excellent all-around play helped lead the Boston Celtics to 11 NBA championships in 13 years, the most prolific championship run in NBA history.

Scorers and Scholars

Sportscaster Tom Brookshier caused a controversy in 1983 when he suggested that the University of Louisville basketball team had a collective IQ of 40. In fact, many basketball stars were as talented in the classroom as they were on the basketball court. Oscar Robertson was a National Honor Student at Crispus Attucks High School in Indianapolis before becoming an All-American at the University of Cincinnati. The NBA's all-time leading scorer, Kareem Abdul-Jabbar, has an IQ of more than 130. Although he never attended college, Kobe Bryant, superstar guard of the Los Angeles Lakers, scored more than 1300 on the SAT.

1. BILL BRADLEY

Bill Bradley was the personification of the scholar-athlete. One of the greatest scorers in college basketball history, he led Princeton of the Ivy League to a Final Four appearance. Selected to be a Rhodes scholar, Bradley delayed his professional basketball career for two years to study at Oxford University. His 10-year pro career with the New York Knicks included two NBA championships. After his playing days were over, Bradley embarked on a political career in which he served as a senator from New Jersey and ran for the Democratic nomination for president in the year 2000.

2. WHIZZER WHITE

Byron "Whizzer" White averaged nearly seven points per game during his basketball career at the University of Colorado and played in the NIT in 1938. A tremendous halfback, White finished second in the Heisman balloting in 1937. He was also the valedictorian of the university. His exceptional academic and athletic record earned him a Rhodes scholarship. White went on to lead the NFL in rushing in 1938 and 1940. In 1962, he was appointed to the United States Supreme Court by President John F. Kennedy.

3. JAMES CASH

James Cash was the first African-American to play basketball in the Southwest Conference. He averaged 13 points and 11 rebounds during his career at Texas Christian University, from 1966 to 1969, and he led the conference in rebounding in his senior year. In 1976, he became the first black tenured professor at Harvard University.

4. DAVE BING

Detroit Pistons guard Dave Bing was the NBA Rookie of the Year in 1967. The next season he won the league scoring title with a 27.1 average. One of the highlights of his twelve-year career was being named MVP at the 1976 NBA All-Star Game. In 1978, he founded Bing Steel. Under his leadership, the company became one of the ten largest African-American-owned businesses in the United States.

5. **ROBERT HOPKINS**

Known for his deadly hook shot, Robert Hopkins scored 3,266 points during his career at Pasadena College from 1951 to 1954. Six times Hopkins scored 40 points or more in a game, and he was twice named to All-American teams. An honor student, he was elected student body president. After his basketball career was over, he became a professor of mathematics and statistics at Biola College in California.

6. **NOLAN ARCHIBALD**

Nolan Archibald averaged more than 25 points per game for Dixie College (Utah) in 1966. After transferring to Weber State, he averaged more than 15 points per game as a junior. A cum laude graduate, Archibald went on to a successful business career that culminated when he became president and CEO of Black & Decker.

7. **MANNIE JACKSON**

Mannie Jackson was born in a boxcar in East St. Louis. During his senior year at the University of Illinois in 1960, Jackson averaged 16.4 points per game. He played basketball with the Harlem Globetrotters and eventually owned the team. Jackson was also a senior vice president at the Honeywell Corporation.

8. **HANK KNOCHE**

Hank Knoche led the Big Seven Conference in scoring with a 16.4-point average while playing for Colorado in 1947. In 1976, Knoche was appointed deputy director of the Central Intelligence Agency.

9. JOHN DICK

A starting forward for the NCAA champion Oregon Ducks in 1939, John Dick led the Pacific Coast Conference in scoring the following year. Dick had a distinguished career in the United States Navy and retired with the rank of admiral.

10. JAMES MARTIN

James Martin averaged seven points and seven rebounds during his basketball career at Auburn University in the early 1950s. In 1984, he became president of the university.

The Write Stuff

G ary Payton, All-Star guard for the Seattle Supersonics, wrote an autobiographical children's book entitled *Confidence Counts*. Payton is the latest basketball player to become an author.

1. CLAIR BEE

Bobby Knight called Clair Bee "the most brilliant mind ever involved in athletics." Bee was elected to the College Basketball Hall of Fame in 1967, and his teams at Rider College lost just seven games in seven years. He coached Long Island University from 1931 to 1951. His teams won the NIT in 1939 and 1941. An innovative coach, he was also a prolific author. Bee wrote 44 books, including 23 books in the Chip Hilton series.

2. PETE GENT

Pete Gent averaged 21 points per game for the Michigan State Spartans during the 1963–64 season. Equally talented at football, Gent played five seasons as a receiver with the Dallas Cowboys. His novel *North Dallas Forty* was a celebrated account of life as a professional football player and was made into a movie starring Nick Nolte. Another of his books, *The Conquering Heroes,* offered a fictional look at college basketball.

3. ALEX ENGLISH

Alex English scored more than 25,000 points during his NBA career. The league scoring champion in 1983 with the Denver Nuggets, English averaged 25 points or more for eight consecutive seasons and was the NBA scoring leader during the 1980s. Living up to his name, English published three volumes of poetry.

4. TOM MESCHERY

Tom Meschery averaged 12.7 points per game during his NBA career, which lasted from 1961 to 1971. He played for Philadelphia, San Francisco, and Seattle. In 1971, he published a book of poetry.

5. MICHAEL CRICHTON

Michael Crichton is the best-selling author of *The Andromeda Strain* and *Jurassic Park.* As a student at Harvard, the 6'8" Crichton averaged six points per game on the freshman basketball team and played on the varsity squad during the 1961–62 season.

6. ROBERT JAMES WALLER

Robert James Waller averaged 14.2 points per game as a guard for Northern Iowa during the 1961–62 season. During the 1990s, he authored the best-selling novels *The Bridges of Madison County* and *Slow Waltz in Cedar Bend.*

7. JOHN WIDEMAN

John Wideman scored more than 13 points a game for the University of Pennsylvania during his junior and senior seasons. A Rhodes scholar, he became a professor of English literature and authored several books, including *Hurry Home* (1966) and *Philadelphia Five* (1990).

8. JERRY LUCAS

Jerry Lucas had a brilliant basketball career, both as a college and pro player. He was twice named college player of the year at Ohio State and led his team to the NCAA title in 1960. He used his photographic memory to be a straight-A student. He played 11 seasons in the NBA, starring for Cincinnati, San Francisco, and New York. He co-authored *The Memory Book,* which sold more than two million copies. Lucas demonstrated his remarkable memory by memorizing the first 500 pages of the New York phone book.

9. TONY LUPIEN

Tony Lupien was the captain of the Harvard basketball team during the 1938–39 season, and he played six seasons as a first baseman with the Boston Red Sox, Philadelphia Phillies, and Chicago White Sox. Lupien co-authored *The Imperfect Diamond,* a book dealing with the baseball reserve clause.

10. JACK RAMSAY

Jack Ramsay's teams at St. John's University compiled a record of 234 wins and 74 losses. His 1961 squad reached the NCAA Final Four. One of the NBA's winningest coaches, he led the Portland Trail Blazers to the NBA championship in 1977. Ramsay, who earned his doctorate degree from the University of Pennsylvania, authored a book on coaching.

High-School Highs

Over the years there have been many extraordinary performances and amazing games in high-school basketball.

1. TOWNS COUNTY HIGH SCHOOL

Rabum County High School defeated Towns County 129–41 in a game played in Clayton, Georgia. What makes the game remarkable is that Towns County scored 56 of its opponents' points. Angry at the officials due to several disputed calls, the Towns County players began shooting at the Rabum County basket in protest.

2. WALTER GARRETT

In 1963, Walter Garrett of Birmingham West End High School scored all of his team's points in a 97–54 victory over Birmingham Glenn Vocational. His point total would have been even greater except that Birmingham Glenn Vocational assigned all five of its players to guard Garrett.

3. **DANNY HEATER**

On January 26, 1960, Danny Heater of Burnsville, West Virginia, scorched the nets for a high-school record 135 points in a victory over a team from Widen, West Virginia. Heater made 53 of 70 field-goal attempts and sank 29 free throws in his record-breaking performance. Heater scored 82 points in the second half alone.

4. **WILT CHAMBERLAIN**

Wilt Chamberlain set an NBA record when he scored 100 points in a 1962 game. Seven years earlier, he scored 90 points while playing for Philadelphia Overbrook High School in a game against Roxborough. Chamberlain would have easily topped the century mark had he not been removed from the game in the third quarter.

5. **SHINNSTON HIGH SCHOOL**

In the most lopsided matchup in high-school history, Shinnston High School defeated Weirton High 136–0 in a game played in West Virginia on January 27, 1918.

6. **CHATTANOOGA EAST HIGH SCHOOL**

Spectators got their money's worth in a game between Chattanooga East High School and Voltewah High in Tennessee. Chattanooga East won the game 38–37 in 16 overtimes.

7. **ERNEST BLOOD**

Ernest Blood was the most successful coach in high-school basketball history. Blood's teams at St. Benedict's Prep in Newark, New Jersey, won 12 state titles. He coached Passaic High School to 159 consecutive victories between 1925 and

1929. Passaic teams were so dominant that they won a dozen games by more than 100 points.

8. BASKIN HIGH SCHOOL

The 159-game winning streak at Passaic High is a record for boys' high school. The overall high-school record belongs to a girls' school, Baskin High, in Louisiana. Between 1947 and 1953, Baskin High won 218 consecutive games and seven straight state titles.

9. CINDY HARMS

Cindy Harms of Allison Bri Stow High School was a one-woman team in a 1984 game against Grundy Center in Iowa. She scored all 67 points in a 67–54 victory.

10. BOB AND PAT TALLENT

Bob Tallent averaged 40 points a game during the 1963–64 season at Maytown High School in Langley, Kentucky. Seven years later, his brother, Pat, proved to be just as talented, as he also posted a 40-point average for Maytown High.

Big Stars from Small Colleges

Michael Jordan played at North Carolina, but not every NBA star went to a school with a storied college basketball tradition. Former New York Knicks' great Walt Frazier attended Southern Illinois University. Prolific scorer World B. Free attended tiny Guilford College in North Carolina. Phil Jackson, the coach of eight NBA champions, played his college basketball at North Dakota.

1. VERN MIKKELSON

Vern Mikkelson was the NBA's first dominant power forward. He starred for the Minneapolis Lakers from 1949 to 1959 and played on four championship teams. Mikkelson attended Hamline College in Minnesota. Until Mikkelson led the school to the NAIA championship in 1949, Hamline's claim to fame was their loss in the first intercollegiate basketball game in 1895.

2. DENNIS RODMAN

Dennis Rodman won seven NBA rebounding titles and was named to the league's All Defensive Team seven times. A late bloomer, Rodman attended Cooke County Junior College in Texas, then transferred to Southwestern Oklahoma State. Rodman led the NAIA in rebounding in 1985 and 1986.

3. SCOTTIE PIPPEN

A teammate of Dennis Rodman on the championship Chicago Bulls squads of the 1990s, Scottie Pippen earned a reputation as professional basketball's best all-around player. He attended high school in Hamburg, Arkansas. He was so lightly regarded at first that he was kept on the squad only because he agreed to double as the team manager. Eventually, Pippen developed into an outstanding player and averaged 23.5 points for Central Arkansas as a college senior in 1987.

4. JOE FULKS

"Jumpin" Joe Fulks was the NBA's first scoring champion. His 23.2 average for the Philadelphia Warriors during the 1946–47 season was more than six points higher than runner-up Bob Feerick's. His 63 points in a game against Indianapolis in 1949 broke the existing league scoring record by 15 points. Fulks's mark would not be surpassed until Elgin Baylor scored 73 points in a game 10 years later. His prolific scoring outburst in the NBA was unexpected. Fulks had averaged only 13 points a game during his college career at Murray State Teachers College.

5. HARRY GALLATIN

Harry "The Horse" Gallatin played in 682 consecutive NBA games, a streak that lasted from 1948 to 1958. The Hall-of-Famer played collegiate basketball at Northeast Missouri State Teachers College.

6. **EARL MONROE**

Earl "The Pearl" Monroe first flashed his brilliance at Winston-Salem State. In his senior year, Monroe averaged 41.5 points per game. Despite playing at a small college, Monroe was selected by the Baltimore Bullets with the second overall pick in the 1967 NBA draft. Monroe immediately justified the selection by averaging 24.3 points and earning Rookie of the Year honors.

7. **JOHN STOCKTON**

John Stockton played college basketball at Gonzaga University in his hometown of Spokane, Washington. He achieved stardom in the NBA with the Utah Jazz. Stockton is the league's all-time assists and steals leader.

8. **LARRY BIRD**

Larry Bird initially enrolled at Indiana University but transferred to Indiana State because he preferred attending a smaller college. Bird averaged more than 30 points per game during his career at Indiana State and led his team to the NCAA finals in 1979. Bird cemented his greatness during his career with the Boston Celtics from 1979 to 1992. Bird was the NBA's MVP in 1984, 1985, and 1986.

9. **ELGIN BAYLOR**

Elgin Baylor was basketball's first skywalker. He averaged 31 points for the College of Idaho in 1955. Transferring to Seattle University, he averaged 32.5 points per game and led his team to the NCAA finals in 1958. Baylor brought his amazing athleticism to the NBA in 1958 and averaged 27.4

points per game during his career with the Lakers before retiring in 1972.

10. **SAM JONES**

The state of North Carolina is known for producing college basketball stars. Numerous players have gone to the NBA from North Carolina, Duke, and Wake Forest, but Sam Jones played his college basketball at little-known North Carolina Central. Drafted by the Boston Celtics in 1957, Jones was so sure that he was not going to make the team that he planned on accepting a job as a high-school teacher. When the high school refused to offer him the $500 salary increase he expected, Jones decided to take a shot at pro basketball. Jones not only made the team, but he helped the Celtics to 10 NBA championships in his 12 seasons in Boston. During the 1964–65 season, Jones averaged nearly 26 points per game.

Basketball Prodigies

Darius Miles, drafted by the Los Angeles Clippers as the third overall pick of the 2000 draft, is the latest high-school player to skip college and go directly to the NBA.

1. MOSES MALONE

Moses Malone played high-school basketball in Petersburg, Virginia. Upon graduation, he was signed by Utah of the ABA. He became the first high-school player to go directly to professional basketball. Malone was named ABA Rookie of the Year in 1975 and joined the NBA in 1976. He led the NBA six times in rebounding and was the league's MVP in 1979, 1982, and 1983. Malone played 21 seasons as a professional.

2. KEVIN GARNETT

Kevin Garnett was drafted by the Minnesota Timberwolves with the fifth pick of the 1995 NBA draft. Garnett had played his high-school ball at the Farragut Academy in Chicago. By the year 2000, Garnett had raised his scoring average to nearly 22 points per game and was voted to the All-NBA First Team.

3. **KOBE BRYANT**

Kobe Bryant was so talented at Lower Merion High School in Pennsylvania that he was drafted out of high school by Charlotte in 1996. The Hornets traded Bryant's rights to the Los Angeles Lakers in exchange for center Vlade Divac. Bryant won the NBA slam dunk competition in 1997 and averaged 22.5 points a game on the 2000 Los Angeles Lakers championship team.

4. **JOE BRENNAN**

In the days before the NBA, numerous professional leagues operated around the country. Joe Brennan went directly from high school to the pros. Because playing professional basketball was not lucrative back then, Brennan kept his day job at the Emigrant Savings Bank in New York. The job was so important to him that he refused to report when he was drafted by Fort Wayne (Indiana) of the American Basketball League in 1925. Brennan was one of the best players of his day and twice led the Brooklyn Visitations to Metropolitan League titles. He refused to go on road trips outside the New York area so that he wouldn't miss work at the bank. Despite this awkward arrangement, Brennan managed to play professional basketball for 16 seasons. His loyalty to the bank was rewarded, and he eventually became a vice president.

5. **TRACY MCGRADY**

Tracy McGrady attended high school at the Mount Zion Christian Academy in Durham, North Carolina. Drafted by the Toronto Raptors in the first round of the 1997 NBA draft, McGrady quickly became one of the best young players in the league.

6. JERMAINE O'NEAL

Jermaine O'Neal played basketball at Eau Claire High School in Columbia, South Carolina. When the 18-year-old played his first professional game with the Portland Trail Blazers on December 5, 1996, he became the youngest player in NBA history.

7. DARRYL DAWKINS

Darryl Dawkins had multiple college scholarship offers after starring at Maynard Evans High School in Orlando, Florida. In 1975, he became the first high-school player ever to be picked in the first round of the NBA draft, when selected by the Philadelphia 76ers. Remembered for his backboard-shattering dunks, Dawkins averaged double figures in scoring from 1978 to 1986 while playing for Philadelphia and New Jersey.

8. JOE GRABOSKI

Joe Graboski did not attend college. In 1948, he joined the Chicago Stags and played in the NBA for 13 seasons. Graboski averaged 14.4 points a game for the NBA champion Philadelphia Warriors in 1956.

9. BILL WILLOUGHBY

Bill Willoughby played prep basketball at Dwight Morrow High School in Englewood, New Jersey. Drafted out of high school by the Atlanta Hawks in the second round of the 1975 draft, Willoughby played eight seasons in the NBA.

10. JONATHAN BENDER

Forward Jonathan Bender played basketball at Picayune Memorial High School in Mississippi. Selected by the Toronto

Raptors in the first round of the 1999 NBA draft, Bender was traded to the Indiana Pacers. There he became teammates with Al Harrington, another young NBA player who did not attend college.

The Greatest College Players

From Hank Luisetti to the stars of today, college basketball has been blessed with some remarkable talents. These 10 players represent the best of the best.

1. LEW ALCINDOR

If Lew Alcindor was not the best college basketball player, he was certainly the most dominant. During his three years with UCLA, the Bruins won 88 of 90 games and three consecutive national championships. He was named college player of the year in 1967 and 1969 and was the Final Four MVP three consecutive years. He averaged 26.4 points per game during his college career and shot 63.9 percent from the field despite the NCAA's ban on the dunk shot, which was later lifted.

2. OSCAR ROBERTSON

John Wooden called Oscar Robertson "the best high-school player I ever saw." Robertson more than lived up to Wooden's expectations as a college player with the University of Cincinnati from 1957 to 1960. Averaging 33.8 points during

Oscar Robertson set 14 NCAA records and led the nation in scoring three consecutive years during his college career at the University of Cincinnati.

his college career, he led the nation in scoring for three years and set 14 NCAA records. The "Big O" was *The Sporting News* college player of the year in 1958, 1959, and 1960.

3. "PISTOL" PETE MARAVICH

The greatest scorer in college basketball history, Pete Maravich averaged 44.2 points per game during his career at Louisiana State University. Twenty-eight times he scored 50 points or more in a game. His numerous college records include the most points scored in a career (3,667) and the highest single-season average (44.5 in 1970). Maravich was named *The Sporting News* college player of the year in 1970.

4. TOM GOLA

A great scorer and rebounder, Tom Gola led LaSalle College to the NIT championship in 1952 and the NCAA title in 1954. His combined total of 4,663 career points and rebounds still remains an NCAA record. A unanimous first-team All-American in 1954 and 1955, he was the national player of the year in 1955.

5. AUSTIN CARR

Notre Dame guard Austin Carr averaged 38 points per game in both 1970 and 1971. He scored 46 points in an upset of UCLA in 1971. His 41.3-point average in the NCAA tournament is a record that still stands. Carr scored 61 points in a 1970 NCAA tournament game against Ohio State. In 1971, Carr was named the national player of the year.

6. BILL WALTON

Bill Walton faced the nearly impossible task of following Lew Alcindor at UCLA, but Walton maintained the Bruins' winning tradition, leading his team to two NCAA titles and 73 consecutive victories. Coach John Wooden called Walton the most fundamentally sound center who ever played the game. The two-time college player of the year averaged more than 20 points per game during his career and shot over 65 percent from the field. His greatest performance came in the 1973 NCAA title game against Memphis State. Walton made 21 of 22 shots and scored 44 points in a 87–66 UCLA victory.

7. BILL RUSSELL

Bill Russell led the University of San Francisco to 60 consecutive wins and NCAA titles in 1955 and 1956. He averaged more than 20 points and 20 rebounds a game during his college career. What made Bill Russell truly great was his defensive wizardry.

8. BILL BRADLEY

Bill Bradley averaged more than 30 points a game for Princeton University from 1962 to 1965. He was named the national player of the year in 1965. That year he led the Ivy League school to a Final Four appearance and was voted the tournament's MVP. He capped off his college career with a 58-point explosion in the consolation game against Wichita State.

9. DAVID THOMPSON

An incredible leaper, David Thompson was a unanimous first-team All-American for three consecutive years at North Carolina State. He averaged nearly 30 points per game and was named college player of the year in 1975. He led North Carolina State to the NCAA title in 1974.

10. **ELVIN HAYES**

Elvin Hayes rivaled Lew Alcindor as the dominant college player of his time. The University of Houston big man averaged 36.8 points and 18.9 rebounds per game during the 1967–68 season. Hayes was recognized as the national college player of the year. In his greatest game, Hayes scored 39 points and outplayed Alcindor in a 71–69 Houston victory.

Elvin Hayes made the University of Houston a basketball powerhouse during the late 1960s. He was the national college player of the year for the 1967–1968 season, beating out Lew Alcindor.

The Greatest Professional Players

O nly the best players are good enough to play professional basketball. These men are among the greatest players in NBA history.

1. WILT CHAMBERLAIN

Wilt Chamberlain set NBA records that will probably never be broken. Wilt "the Stilt" averaged 50.4 points per game with the Philadelphia Warriors during the 1961–62 season, a scoring mark no one else has ever approached. Forty-five times that season, he scored 50 or more points in a game. He topped the 50 mark an unbelievable 118 times in his career. He scored an outstanding 100 points in a game, eclipsing his own single-game scoring record by 22 points. The next season, he averaged 44.8 points per game. Seven times he led the NBA in scoring. The league's all-time leading rebounder, he led the NBA in that department 11 times. Chamberlain holds the single-game record with a 55-rebound performance against the Boston Celtics on November 24, 1960. His 27.2 average during that season is also a record. Chamberlain was the NBA's MVP four times. The 7'1" center proved he could do it all by leading the NBA in assists during the 1967–68 season. In 1973, his final year in the NBA, Chamberlain set a field-goal-percentage record by making 72.7 percent of his shots.

2. OSCAR ROBERTSON

Oscar Robertson was the greatest all-around player in NBA history. Six years he averaged more than 30 points per game while playing for the Cincinnati Royals. During the 1961–62 season, Robertson averaged a triple double with 30.8 points, 12.5 rebounds, and 11.4 assists per game. In fact, his cumulative average for the years 1961 though 1965 were 30.3 points, 10.4 rebounds, and 10.6 assists per game. Selected to the NBA All First Team nine consecutive seasons, Robertson was the league MVP in 1964.

3. MICHAEL JORDAN

There are many who consider Michael Jordan the greatest basketball player who ever lived. In fact, an ESPN poll ranked Jordan at the greatest athlete of the twentieth century. Jordan led the Chicago Bulls to six NBA titles during the 1990s. He led the NBA in scoring 10 times, and his 31.5 career average tops even Wilt Chamberlain. Five times he was voted the league's MVP, and he was selected to the NBA All Defensive Team on nine separate occasions. One of the game's most exciting players, he helped the NBA reach new heights in popularity.

4. KAREEM ABDUL-JABBAR

Kareem Abdul-Jabbar was a 19-time NBA All-Star, and six times he was named the league's MVP. He played on six NBA championship teams, once with the Milwaukee Bucks

Wilt Chamberlain, *center,* grabs another rebound while Bill Russell, *left,* his great rival, looks on. Chamberlain's NBA scoring and rebounding numbers are mind-blowing. He is the only NBA player to score 100 points in a game, and his prolific 50.4 points-per-game average during the 1960–1961 season is the best ever. His 27.2 rebounds per game that same season is also a record.

and five more times as a member of the Los Angeles Lakers. His 38,387 career points are easily the most in NBA history.

5. BILL RUSSELL

Bill Russell was basketball's consummate winner. His Boston Celtics won the NBA title 11 times during his 13-year career. Russell led the league in rebounding five times. He was voted MVP in 1958, 1961, 1963, and 1965. Russell was probably the greatest defensive player in basketball history.

6. JERRY WEST

Jerry West was one of the greatest shooters in NBA history. The sharpshooting guard averaged 27.0 points per game during his career and led the NBA in scoring during the 1969–70 season with a 31.2 average. He earned the nickname "Mr. Clutch" for his outstanding performances in the playoffs. His 29.1 career playoff average ranks second to Michael Jordan.

7. LARRY BIRD

Larry Bird averaged 24.3 points per game from 1979 to 1992. One of the best three-point shooters in the game, Bird won the long-distance-shootout competition at the All-Star games in 1986, 1987, and 1988. His 88.6 percent career free-throw average is one of the top five in league history. Bird led the Celtics to three NBA championships in the 1980s. A three-time MVP, Bird's ability to come through in the clutch made him a legend in Boston.

8. ELGIN BAYLOR

Elgin Baylor averaged 27.4 points per game during his career with the Lakers, from 1958 to 1972. Known as "The Man of

Larry Bird was a masterful outside shooter and clutch player for the Celtics. He helped them win three NBA championships during the 1980s, becoming the most beloved player in the Celtics' history in the process.

a Thousand Moves," Baylor averaged 38.3 points during the 1961–62 season. An excellent rebounder, Baylor averaged nearly 20 boards per game during the 1960–61 season. His incredible leaping ability and athletic play made him the game's first modern player.

9. JOHN STOCKTON AND KARL MALONE

John Stockton and Karl Malone have played together with the Utah Jazz since 1985. The two All-Stars are so linked that it's difficult to imagine one without the other. Stockton is the all-time career leader in assists and steals. He led the NBA in assists for nine consecutive years from 1988 to 1996.

Malone, the quintessential power forward, became the NBA's number two all-time leading scorer in 2000. "The Mailman" was the NBA's MVP in 1997 and 1999.

10. BOB PETTIT

Bob Pettit averaged 26.4 points and 16.2 rebounds during his 11-year NBA career with the Hawks. Pettit led the NBA in scoring in 1956 and 1959 and both years was voted the league's MVP.

The Greatest College Teams

I n the history of college basketball, these teams stand out.

1. **1968 UCLA**

The UCLA Bruins won three NCAA titles and compiled an 88-2 record from 1967 to 1969, the three seasons Lew Alcindor played center. The 1967 team, without a senior on the roster, went undefeated in 30 games. The 1969 team went 29-1 and defeated Purdue by 20 points in the title game. The 1968 Bruins lost only once, a 71–69 game against Houston in which Alcindor was hampered by an eye injury. The Bruins avenged the loss in the NCAA semifinal when they blew out Houston 101–69. Alcindor headed a formidable lineup that included Lucius Allen, Mike Warren, Lynn Shackelford, and Mike Lynn.

2. **1972 UCLA**

The Bill Walton era at UCLA was nearly as dominant as the Alcindor years. The Bruins went undefeated in 1972 and 1973. The 1972 team was particularly strong, with an average margin of victory of more than 30 points a game. Besides Walton, the team featured guards Henry Bibby and Greg Lee and for-wards Keith Wilkes and Larry Farmer.

3. 1956 SAN FRANCISCO

San Francisco, led by center Bill Russell, won back-to-back national championships in 1955 and 1956. The Dons won 60 consecutive games and led the nation in defense for two straight seasons. The supporting cast for Russell included guards K. C. Jones and Hal Perry and forwards Carl Boldt and Mike Farmer.

4. 1976 INDIANA

Often cited as the greatest college team of all time, the 1976 Indiana Hoosiers won all 32 games despite playing an ex-tremely difficult schedule. Led by forward Scott May and cen-ter Kent Benson, the Hoosiers defeated St. John's, Alabama, Marquette, UCLA, and Michigan in the NCAA tournament en route to the title. The deep squad also featured forward Tom Abernathy and guards Quinn Buckner and Bobby Wilkerson.

5. 1957 NORTH CAROLINA

North Carolina capped its undefeated 1957 season with a triple-overtime victory in the NCAA championship game against a Kansas team led by Wilt Chamberlain. The tena-cious Tar Heels had won the semifinal game against Michi-gan State in three overtimes. Star forward Lenny Rosenbluth led the team with a 28-point average. The starting five also included forward Pete Brennan, center Joe Quigg, and guards Tommy Kearns and Bob Cunningham.

6. 1982 NORTH CAROLINA

For sheer talent, it would be hard to top the 1982 North Carolina national champions. Michael Jordan was only the team's third-highest scorer, behind forward James Worthy and center Sam Perkins. Forward Matt Doherty and guard Jimmy Black rounded out the starting five.

7. **1962 CINCINNATI**

The Cincinnati Bearcats won back-to-back national championships in 1961 and 1962 and came within a basket of winning in 1963. In the 1961 and 1962 championship games, Cincinnati defeated an incredibly talented team from Ohio State that featured Jerry Lucas and John Havlicek. The balanced Bearcat team consisted of center Paul Hogue, forwards Ron Bonham and George Wilson, and guards Tom Thacker and Tony Yates.

8. **1960 OHIO STATE**

Ohio State advanced to the NCAA title game three consecutive years beginning in 1960. The Buckeyes defeated defending national champion California 75–55 in the 1960 championship game, becoming the first team to win all of its tournament games by more than 15 points. The starting five were center Jerry Lucas, forwards John Havlicek and Joe Roberts, and guards Larry Siegfried and Mel Nowell. Bobby Knight also played for the Buckeyes in a backup role.

9. **1974 NORTH CAROLINA STATE**

The 1974 North Carolina State team won 30 games and lost only one. The team had been undefeated the previous year but was on probation and had been barred from competing in the NCAA tournament. The Wolfpack defeated UCLA 80–77 in double overtime in the NCAA semifinals to end the Bruins' six-year reign as national champions. They capped off their season with a 76–64 victory over Marquette in the championship game. The Wolfpack was led by the fantastic

David Thompson, who averaged 26 points during the season. Other stars on the team included towering center Tom Burleson and tiny guard Monte Towe. Also playing prominent roles were guard Moe Rivers and forwards Phil Spence and Tim Stoddard, a future major-league baseball pitcher.

10. 1992 DUKE

Duke won 34 games in 1992, culminating with a 71–51 romp over Michigan's "Fab Five" in the NCAA championship game. Duke's 104–103 overtime victory against Kentucky in the regional finals is widely considered the greatest game in college basketball history. The Blue Devils' starting lineup consisted of center Christian Laettner, forwards Grant Hill and Thomas Hill, and guards Bobby Hurley and Billy McCaffrey.

Fab Fives

These college teams are remembered for their distinctive nicknames.

1. FABULOUS FIVE

Of Kentucky's many storied teams, The Fabulous Five hold a special place in the hearts of fans. The Wildcats dominated college basketball in the late 1940s. Over a three-year period, they won 102 games and lost eight, clinching national championships in 1948 and 1949. Kentucky's Fabulous Five were Alex Groza, Ralph Beard, Wallace "Wah Wah" Jones, Cliff Barker, and Ken Rollins.

2. PHI SLAMMA JAMMA

The Houston Cougars were upset by North Carolina State on a last-second shot in the 1983 NCAA title game. The Cougars, led by future NBA stars Hakeem Olajuwon and Clyde Drexler, were known as Phi Slamma Jamma for their above-the-rim style of play.

The University of Houston's 1983 team, nicknamed Phi Slamma Jamma for its above-the-rim play, was a memorable team to watch. It was led by future NBA stars Hakeem Olajuwon, *above,* and Clyde Drexler, *following page.*

Clyde Drexler.

3. **FAB FIVE**

Michigan started five freshman in 1992, and the Fab Five reached the NCAA championship game. The outstanding recruiting class included Chris Webber, Juwan Howard, and Jalen Rose. The Fab Five lost to Duke in the 1992 NCAA finals and to North Carolina in the 1993 championship game.

4. **BLITZ KIDS**

Utah won the 1944 NCAA title despite the team's starting five averaging barely six feet in height and 18 years in age. On top of that, all five were freshman. The squad included Arnie Ferrin, Herb Wilkinson, Wat Misaka, Bob Lewis, Dick Smuin, Bill Kastelic, and sophomore Fred Sheffield. They were known as The Blitz Kids for their whirlwind style of play.

5. **WHIZ KIDS**

The 1943 Illinois team went 17-1 and was known as The Whiz Kids. They received the name after radio personality Grayce Hewlett remarked, "Those kids really whiz down the floor." The Whiz Kids were Andy Phillip, Art Mathisen, Jack Smiley, Gene Vance, and Ken Menke. The team did not compete in the NCAA or NIT because the players enlisted in the military.

6. **TALL TIMBERS**

Oregon won its only basketball national title in 1939 with a team known alternately as The Tall Timbers or The Tall Firs. The squad was led by 6'8" center Slim Wintermute and forwards Laddie Gale and John Dick. The Tall Timbers, who got their nickname from a Portland sports editor, defeated Ohio State 46–33 in the NCAA title game.

7. **RUPP'S RUNTS**

The 1966 Kentucky team was known as Rupp's Runts because none of the starters were taller than 6'5". Coach Adolph Rupp's squad included Pat Riley, Louie Dampier, Thad Jaracz, Larry Conley, and Tommy Kron. Rupp's Runts reached the NCAA championship game but lost to Texas Western 72–65.

8. **FIDDLIN' FIVE**

The 1958 Kentucky team was known as The Fiddlin' Five. The name originated after Coach Rupp observed, "They keep fiddlin' around and fiddlin' around, then finally pulling it out at the end." The Fiddlin' Five were Vern Hatton, Johnny Cox, John Crigler, Adrian Smith, and Ed Beck. The team lost six games during the season, the most a Kentucky team had lost in 15 years, but they defeated a Seattle University team led by Elgin Baylor in the NCAA championship game 84–72.

9. **WONDER FIVE**

Center Matty Begovich, forwards Max Posnack and Mac Kinsbrunner, and guards Allie Schuckman and Rip Gerson formed the starting lineup of a celebrated St. John's team of the late 1920s known as The Wonder Five. The team, coached by James Freeman, compiled a record of 86 wins and eight losses over a four-year period that included a 27-game winning streak. The team was celebrated for its disciplined offense and tenacious defense. The Wonder Five's success helped popularize the game of basketball in New York City.

10. **ROCKET EIGHT**

The 1955 Alabama basketball team coached by Johnny Dee was called The Rocket Eight, named after a high-performance automobile manufactured by Oldsmobile. The squad included Jerry Harper, George Linn, Dennis O'Shea, Leon Marlaire, Dick Gunder, Billy Crews, Dick Wise, and Jim Bratton. Alabama was ranked fifth in the final polls but did not play in the post-season tournaments because of a rules infraction concerning the eligibility of players two years earlier.

Hick, Brick, and Tricky Dick

These players had nicknames they'd rather forget.

1. TRICKY DICK

Before Richard Nixon was saddled with the derisive nickname "Tricky Dick," it belonged to basketball star Dick McGuire. He played with the New York Knicks and Detroit Pistons from 1949 to 1960 and was consistently among the league leaders in assists. McGuire earned the moniker because his passing skills so befuddled the opposition.

2. PIGGY

Ward Lambert retired in 1946 with a 371-152 record in 29 seasons as basketball coach at Purdue. Lambert was one of the first college coaches to play an up-tempo style of basketball. He was nicknamed Piggy because he wore his hair in pigtails as a youth.

3. TIMBER

Ralph Siewert, one of the NBA's first seven-footers, was nicknamed "Sky" during his college days at Dakota Wesleyan. He played 21 games for the St. Louis Bombers during the 1946–47 season. In St. Louis, fans called Siewert "Timber" because he fell like a tree when he was knocked to the floor by stronger players.

4. BRICK

Brick is the term used for a shot that doesn't even come close to going into the basket. John "Brick" Breeden played guard for Montana State and later coached the team to seven Rocky Mountain Conference championships.

5. HERMAN MUNSTER

Kevin McHale starred for the Boston Celtics from 1980 to 1993. One of the best post players in basketball, he was selected as one of the 50 greatest players in NBA history in 1996. The 6'10" McHale was given the nickname "Herman Munster" by Mychal Thompson when they were teammates at the University of Minnesota. The nickname comes from the Frankenstein-like character Herman Munster, played by Fred Gwynne in the 1960s sitcom *The Munsters.*

6. HICK FROM FRENCH LICK

McHale's Boston Celtics teammate Larry Bird was called "The Hick from French Lick" because he was a country boy who hailed from French Lick, Indiana. Bird preferred the nickname given to him by appreciative Celtic fans, "Larry Legend."

7. ZEKE FROM CABIN CREEK

Jerry West was given the nickname "Zeke from Cabin Creek" by Los Angeles Lakers teammate Elgin Baylor. West had grown up in West Virginia near a town called Cabin Creek.

Baylor arrived at Zeke because it sounded like a hillbilly name to him. West's ability to make a big play when it was most needed earned him a more accurate nickname, "Mr. Clutch."

8. THE WORM

Dennis Rodman was given the nickname "The Worm" because of the way he wriggled when playing pinball as a youth. The nickname also described the way he maneuvered his way to the basket to get into position for a rebound. Rodman wormed his way to seven NBA rebounding crowns.

9. TOMMY GUN

In basketball, a player who shoots too often is known as a gunner. Tom Heinsohn played for the Boston Celtics from 1956 to 1965 and earned the nickname "Tommy Gun" because he rarely passed up a shot, firing the ball from every conceivable angle. Heinsohn made enough of them to be elected to the Basketball Hall of Fame in 1986.

10. MACHINE GUN

Travis Grant was the first college player to score more than 4,000 points in a career. Nicknamed "Machine Gun" because he was a scoring machine, the Kentucky State star notched 4,045 points and averaged 33.4 points per game. He once made 35 baskets during a 75-point performance against Northwest Institute. Grant was so accurate that his 63.8 percent field-goal percentage set a Division II record.

Magic Men

Sometimes a basketball nickname can become more famous than a player's given name.

1. MAGIC

Earvin Johnson played basketball at Everett High School in Lansing, Michigan. In one 1974 game, Johnson had 36 points, 18 rebounds, 16 assists, and 20 steals, a rare quadruple double. Fred Stanley, a local newspaper writer, described Johnson's play as being like magic. Johnson lived up to his nickname by leading Michigan State to the NCAA title in 1979 and brought "showtime" to five NBA-champion Los Angeles Lakers teams.

2. MAILMAN

Karl Malone was nicknamed "The Mailman" by a sportswriter during his college days at Louisiana Tech because he always delivered. Malone made enough deliveries to the hoop as a member of the Utah Jazz to become the NBA's second all-time leading scorer.

3. ICEMAN

George Gervin got his nickname, "The Iceman," when he played for the Virginia Squires of the ABA in 1973. Squires guard Fatty Taylor first called him "Iceberg Slim" after a pimp. The nickname evolved into "The Iceman," which perfectly described Gervin's cool, composed manner on the court.

4. PEARL

Earl Monroe was called "Black Magic" during his early days on the playgrounds of Philadelphia. It wasn't until his college years at Winston-Salem State that Monroe received the nickname "The Pearl" when a sportswriter began to refer to his incredible moves as "pearls." Monroe had enough pearls to average 41.5 points per game during his senior season in 1967.

5. STILT

Wilt Chamberlain was called "The Big Dipper" because of his patented finger-roll shot. Sportswriters also began calling him "The Stilt," an obvious nickname for the 7′1″ scoring champion. Although Chamberlain detested it, the nickname stuck.

6. THE OWL WITHOUT A VOWEL

One of basketball's most intriguing nicknames belonged to Bill Mlkvy. Because he played for the Temple Owls and did not have a vowel in his last name (unless you count the sometimes vowel "y"), he was nicknamed "The Owl Without a Vowel." Mlkvy led the nation in scoring in 1951 with a 29.1-point average and once scored 73 points in a game.

7. AIR

Michael Jordan was nicknamed "Air Jordan" because of his amazing hang time. Jordan carried professional basketball to new heights of popularity with his fantastic skills.

8. HOUDINI OF THE HARDWOOD

Bill Cousy was nicknamed "The Houdini of the Hardwood" during his college career at Holy Cross. Cousy was a magician with the basketball. His spectacular ball handling, no-look passes, and behind-the-back dribbling made him one of the game's premier attractions and one of the best play-makers in basketball history.

9. KANGAROO KID

Billy Cunningham dispelled the myth that white men can't jump. Nicknamed "The Kangaroo Kid" for his leaping ability, he averaged more than 20 points and 10 rebounds a game during his professional career with the Philadelphia 76ers of the NBA and the Carolina Cougars of the ABA. A knee injury grounded him in 1976 at the age of 32.

10. INDIA RUBBER MAN

A three-time All-American at Purdue from 1930 to 1932, John Wooden was nicknamed "The India Rubber Man" because he dove for a lot of balls and seemed to bounce off the floor. Years later he earned the moniker "The Wizard of Westwood" when he coached the UCLA Bruins to 10 national championships.

The Name Game

The following players had names that made them naturals to play basketball.

1. TONY DUNKIN

The dunk is basketball's most dynamic shot. Tony Dunkin played college basketball for Coastal Carolina and was named the Big South Conference player of the year in 1993.

2. TOM GOLA

Few players were better at scoring field goals than Tom Gola. He made 904 of them as a three-time All-American at LaSalle. Gola added another 2,904 during his NBA career.

3. BOBBY JOE HOOPER

If anyone ever had a nickname suitable for a hoops star, it was Bobby Joe Hooper. The guard played his college ball at Dayton and then spent the 1968–69 season with Indiana of the ABA. Hooper averaged five points a game for the Pacers.

4. JOHN BLOCK

John Block was a 6′9″ forward who played college basketball at the University of Southern California and pro ball from 1966 to 1976. Although blocked shots were not an official NBA stat until 1973, he did block 35 shots in the 1974 season and 32 more in 1975.

5. JOHN TRAPP

One of the most effective defensive maneuvers is the trap. John Trapp played at Nevada-Las Vegas before beginning his six-year NBA career with San Diego in 1968. He was no master of the trap, though, leading the NBA in personal fouls with 337 during the 1970–71 season.

6. MICHAEL CAGE

Basketball players used to be called cagers because the court was enclosed in a cage during the game's early years. Michael Cage played at San Diego State before being drafted by the Los Angeles Clippers in 1984. He averaged 15.7 points per game for the Clippers in 1987.

7. PRESS MARAVICH

The full-court press is one of basketball's toughest defenses. Press Maravich played professional basketball for Youngstown and Pittsburgh from 1945 to 1947. He coached his son, Pete Maravich, during his record-breaking basketball career at Louisiana State. In fact, Pistol Pete's middle name was Press.

8. NEAL WALK

A walk is another name for a traveling violation. Neal Walk played in the NBA from 1969 to 1977. No one knows how many times the 6′10″ player was whistled for walking with the ball, but he did average more than 20 points a game for the Phoenix Suns during the 1972–73 season.

9. JEROME LANE

Jerome Lane played for the University of Pittsburgh and later for the Denver Nuggets during the 1988–89 season. The 6′6″, 230-pound forward spent a lot of time in the lane, pulling down 200 rebounds for Denver.

10. CALVIN FOWLER

Calvin Fowler played guard for Carolina of the ABA during the 1969–70 season. Fowler committed 156 fouls in 78 games and lived up to his name by fouling out of two games.

Colleges That never Won the nCAA

Wyoming and Oklahoma A & M both won the NCAA tournament, but many of basketball's most successful programs have never won national titles.

1. ST. JOHN'S

St John's has been a basketball powerhouse since the glory days of The Wonder Five in the late 1920s. Despite having had coaching greats Joe Lapchick, Frank McGuire, and Lou Carnesecca in charge of the program, St. John's has never won the NCAA tournament. The school did reach the Final Four in 1952 and 1985. Between 1943 and 1989, St. John's won the NIT five times.

2. HOUSTON

Houston went to the Final Four in 1967, 1968, 1982, 1983, and 1984. The Cougars had the misfortune of having their great Elvin Hayes teams of the late 1960s competing against Lew Alcindor's invincible UCLA squads. With stars such as Hakeem Olajuwan and Clyde Drexler, Houston reached the Final Four three consecutive years from 1982 to 1984 but never came away with the big prize.

3. PURDUE

The program at Purdue has been one of the most successful in college basketball history. Some of the great players who have played for the Boilermakers include Charles "Stretch" Murphy, John Wooden, Terry Dischinger, Dave Schellhase, Rick Mount, and Glenn Robinson. Purdue reached the Final Four in 1980 and the championship game in 1969 but has never won the title. Before the NCAA tournament existed, several Purdue teams coached by Piggy Lambert may have been the best in the country.

4. DEPAUL

DePaul has been a perennial basketball power for more than 50 years. In the mid 1940s, DePaul's George Mikan became one of college basketball's first superstars. Over the years, All-Americans such as Mark Aguirre and Terry Cummings have been unable to lead the Blue Demons to the national title. Under legendary coach Ray Meyer, DePaul reached the Final Four in 1943 and 1979.

5. SYRACUSE

Syracuse has twice reached the NCAA title game but has yet to win a national title. The Orangemen lost a heartbreaker in the 1987 NCAA championship game when Keith Smart hit a 15-foot jumper with five seconds remaining to give Indiana a 74–73 victory. Nine years later, Syracuse once again reached the title game but lost to Kentucky.

6. NOTRE DAME

Notre Dame may be best known for its football program, but the school has also had many outstanding basketball teams throughout the years. All-Americans who have played for the Fighting Irish include Austin Carr and Adrian Dantley. Only once, in 1978, did Notre Dame reach the Final Four.

7. LOUISIANA STATE

Some of the best players in basketball history have played at Louisiana State University, including Bob Pettit, Pete Maravich, and Shaquille O'Neal. The Tigers reached the Final Four in 1953, 1981, and 1986 but have never won the title.

8. ILLINOIS

Like Purdue, the University of Illinois is a Big Ten power that has never won an NCAA title, despite the efforts of coaching greats Harry Combes and Lou Henson. The Fighting Illini reached the Final Four in 1949, 1951, 1952, and 1989.

9. TEMPLE

Long a dominant team in the East, Temple won NIT titles in 1938 and 1969. The Owls reached the Final Four in 1956 and 1958 but have never won the NCAA tournament.

10. PROVIDENCE

Providence is another basketball power from the East that has not yet claimed a national championship. Twice the Friars won the NIT. They made it to the NCAA Final Four in 1973 and 1987 but failed to reach the championship game.

Coaches Who Never Won the NCAA

J ohn Chaney of Temple and Purdue's Gene Keady are two college coaching greats who have never guided their teams to national titles. Surprisingly, many coaching legends were never able to add an NCAA title to their resumes.

1. RAY MEYER

Ray Meyer coached basketball at DePaul University from 1942 to 1984. During that period, DePaul won 724 games and lost only 354. Meyer's teams had 20 20-win seasons and played in the NCAA tournament 13 times. The Blue Demons did reach the Final Four in 1979, but they lost to Indiana State 76–74 in the semifinals.

2. JOE LAPCHICK

Joe Lapchick compiled a record of 335 wins and 129 losses as a coach at St. John's from 1936 to 1965, garnering NIT titles in 1943, 1944, 1959, and 1965. During the 1940s, the NIT was more prestigious than the NCAA, and because the tournament was played in New York City, St. John's was, in essence, always the home team. In fact, during Lapchick's tenure, St. John's played only one time in the NCAA tournament, a first-round loss in 1961.

3. LOU CARNESECCA

Lou Carnesecca took over for Joe Lapchick in 1965 and coached St. John's until 1992. During that time, his teams won 526 games and lost 200. Carnesecca's 1985 team won 31 games and advanced to the Final Four. The next season, St. John's won 31 games again but lost in the second round of the NCAA tournament.

4. GUY LEWIS

Probably no coach had more disappointments in the NCAA tournament than Houston's Guy Lewis. He was head coach at Houston from 1956 to 1986. Five times his Cougars reached the Final Four, and twice they played in the championship game. His biggest disappointment came in 1983 when the heavily favored Cougars lost in the finals to North Carolina State 54–52 on a last-second shot. Lewis's record at Houston was 592 wins and 279 losses.

5. EDDIE SUTTON

Eddie Sutton won more than 600 games during his coaching career, which began in 1969 with Creighton. Sutton coached at Creighton, Arkansas, Kentucky, and Oklahoma State, and he took each to the NCAA tournament, making him the only coach to go to the tournament with four different schools. His 1978 Arkansas team reached the Final Four but lost to eventual champion Kentucky in the semifinal game.

6. **LEFTY DRIESELL**

Lefty Driesell coached Davidson, Maryland, and James Madison to appearances in the NCAA tournament. At Maryland, his teams won 20 or more games 10 times. Although his teams were often considered legitimate contenders for the national title, none advanced beyond the third round. Maryland did win the NIT in 1972.

7. **NORM STEWART**

Norm Stewart won more than 700 games as a coach at Northern Iowa and the University of Missouri. One of his best teams was his 1994 squad at Missouri. The Tigers won 28 games and were 14-0 in the Big Eight Conference but lost in the fourth round of the NCAA tournament to Arizona.

8. **RALPH MILLER**

Ralph Miller compiled a 675-382 record in 38 seasons as a coach at Wichita State, Iowa, and Oregon State. Miller was voted national coach of the year in 1981 and 1982. His 1981 team at Oregon State won its first 26 games but lost in the first round of the NCAA tournament to Kansas State. Miller's teams never advanced beyond the third round of the tournament.

9. **JIM BOEHEIM**

Jim Boeheim took over as the Syracuse coach in 1976 and has racked up more than 550 victories in the last quarter century. His team reached the NCAA title game in 1987 but lost to Indiana 74–73. In 1996, Boeheim's Orangemen once again played in the championship game but fell to Kentucky.

10. PETE CARRIL

Pete Carril won more than 500 games at Princeton without the benefit of athletic scholarships. The Ivy League university, known more for its academic excellence than for its sports programs, doesn't give out athletic scholarships, making recruiting top stars difficult. Carril's teams befuddled the opposition with back-door passes and an incredibly patient offense. Princeton won the NIT championship in 1975. In the opening round of the 1996 NCAA tournament, the thirteenth-seeded Tigers upset the defending national champion UCLA Bruins 43–41, one of many upsets pulled by Carril's teams.

Coaching Characters

E very coach has his own formula for success, but even the best-laid plans can go astray. As a New Mexico State coach once said, "We've got a great bunch of outside shooters. Unfortunately, all of our games are played indoors."

1. JOE LAPCHICK

Joe Lapchick was as well known for his eccentricity as for his coaching success. During the 1944 NIT championship game against DePaul, the St. John's coach leaped up off the bench and then fainted. Lapchick later recalled that his team was behind when he fainted and ahead when he regained consciousness. His fainting spells continued during his time as an NBA coach with the New York Knicks. He fainted during games, in the clubhouse, and even when he was advising a player, Tommy Byrnes, that he had been cut. He was so nervous that he tore the lining of his sportscoats to shreds without even knowing it. In response to a questionable call, he once threw a tray of water cups into the air and was drenched. Another time, he had a crying spell after the Knicks blew a 12-point lead. Lapchick frequently threw his sportscoat, sometimes into the faces of spectators behind the bench. A superstitious man, he wore the same shirt during a long winning streak at St. John's. When the streak was finally over, Lapchick's wife picked up the smelly shirt with ice tongs and threw it into the garbage.

2. HENRY CARLSON

Henry Carlson coached the University of Pittsburgh from 1922 to 1953, and his teams were national champions in 1928 and 1930. His deliberate play was personified by his inverted Figure-8 offense, a weave pattern that allowed his team to control the ball. His emotional outbursts and stall tactics frequently drew the ire of fans on the road. Carlson sometimes threw peanuts at hostile fans. He was once beaten with an umbrella by a woman during a game. After a questionable call, Carlson shouted, "This burns me up." Fans responded by dousing him with a bucket of ice water. During a 1938 game against Kentucky, all the calls seemed to be going against him. Carlson gathered up the team's equipment and presented it to Kentucky coach Adolph Rupp. "These officials are giving you everything," he explained. "You might as well take this, too."

3. FRANK KEANEY

Frank Keaney was one of the first coaches to employ a fast-break offense. His "point-a-minute" teams at Rhode Island helped to revolutionize the college game. Years before Bobby Knight threw a chair onto the floor during a game, Keaney flung chairs, towels—anything he could grab—onto the court in disgust. On one occasion when a player fouled out, Keaney placed a chair on the court. "That's my fifth player," he informed the ref. "You can call fouls on him."

4. JESS NEELY

In 1939, Clemson basketball coach Jess Neely turned down an invitation to play in the NIT. The reason is that Neely was also the Clemson football coach, and he did not want his football players who were also on the basketball team to miss practice.

5. BOB DAVIES

Bob Davies coached Seton Hall to a 24-3 record during the 1947 season. What made this accomplishment especially impressive is that he was simultaneously playing pro basketball for the Rochester Royals of the National Basketball League. The arrangement must have agreed with Davies, as he was voted the league's MVP.

6. PHOG ALLEN

Forrest Allen was given the nickname "Phog" because of his foghorn voice. Allen compiled a 746-264 record during his coaching career, which lasted from 1905 to 1956. The culmination of Allen's career was a NCAA title with Kansas in 1952. Allen tried to convince John Wooden to play for Kansas by offering him a job pouring concrete in the school's new football stadium. Wooden declined and enrolled at Purdue. Allen was concerned about seven-foot players such as Bob Kurland dominating the game and unsuccessfully proposed that the basket be raised to 12 feet. Ironically, Wilt Chamberlain enrolled in Kansas just as Allen was about to retire. Allen was so impressed with Wilt that he said that Kansas would win the national title with a lineup of "Chamberlain, two sorority girls, and two Phi Beta Kappas." Kansas, with Chamberlain, reached the NCAA championship game in 1957 but lost to North Carolina in three overtimes.

7. **ADOLPH RUPP**

Adolph Rupp coached the University of Kentucky basketball team from 1930 to 1972. Rupp's team won 875 games and four national titles. The Baron was a perfectionist. He chewed out one of his players, Jack Parkinson, for allowing the man he was guarding to score four points in a 75–6 rout of Arkansas State. In 1941, guard Vince Splane left the team to attend his grandmother's funeral. When he returned, Rupp lectured his players at practice. "We're not going to have any more of this grandmother dying business," he said. In 1934, Jack Tucker missed several free throws in a game against Cincinnati. To teach him a lesson, Rupp made Tucker sit in a chair at the foul line and stare at the basket.

8. **DOC MEANWELL**

Walter "Doc" Meanwell coached Wisconsin to undefeated seasons in 1912 and 1914. Meanwell hated the dribble. His offense was based on short passes. In 1927, Meanwell convinced the Collegiate Rules Committee to make dribbling illegal. Fortunately, they reconsidered and reinstated the dribble.

9. **JOHNNY DEE**

Alabama coach Johnny Dee was upset when his famed 1955 Rocket Eight team was trailing by 13 points at halftime in a game against Georgia Tech. He emphasized his displeasure by punching his fist through a blackboard. He was so disgusted that he stayed in the locker room for the second half. Only after his team regained the lead late in the game did Dee return to the bench. Alabama won 76–72.

Basketball Hall of Fame, Springfield, Mass.

Adolph Rupp, the ornery coach of the University of Kentucky, coached for an amazing forty-two years. He guided Kentucky to four national championships and 875 wins.

10. **BILLY TUBBS**

Oklahoma coach Billy Tubbs found a creative way to criticize the officials in a game against Missouri on February 9, 1989. Sooner fans began throwing objects onto the court after a series of questionable calls. Tubbs asked for the microphone in an apparent attempt to calm the crowd. Tubbs said, "The referees asked that, regardless of how terrible the officiating is, please don't throw things on the floor." Tubbs was given a technical foul, but Oklahoma won the game 112–105.

Women Stars

Women's basketball has progressed rapidly during the last 20 years. For half a century, the women's game was stifled by rules that limited athleticism. Once the rules were changed, these women showed what they could really do.

1. CHERYL MILLER

Cheryl Miller once scored 105 points in a high-school game, and the 6′ 3″ forward notched a total of 3,405 points during her high-school career. A four-time All-American, Miller averaged 23.6 points per game for the University of Southern California from 1982 to 1986. Her outstanding play helped establish the popularity of women's basketball. Cheryl's brother Reggie is a star player with the Indiana Pacers, and her brother Darrell played major-league baseball with the California Angels.

2. LYNETTE WOODARD

Lynette Woodard scored 3,649 points during her career at Kansas from 1977 to 1981. Her total was only 18 points short of the total scored by the men's all-time leader, Pete

Maravich. Woodard made headlines when she became the first woman to play with the Harlem Globetrotters, scoring seven points in her debut on November 13, 1985.

3. nancy LIEBERMAn-CLInE

Nancy Lieberman-Cline played on two national championship teams at Old Dominion. The 1980 national player of the year was popular for her fantastic passing and fancy play. Turning professional, she averaged 32 points per game with the Dallas Diamonds of the WBL (Women's Professional Basketball League).

4. CAROL BLAZEJOWSKI

Carol Blazejowski had the best jump shot in women's basketball. She set a women's scoring record by averaging 38.6 points for Montclair State during the 1977–78 season. Her career average of 31.7 is also a record.

5. LUSIA HARRIS

In 1992, Lusia Harris became the first woman player inducted into the Basketball Hall of Fame. One of the first women superstars in basketball, she averaged 25.9 points per game during her college career at Delta State from 1973 to 1977. Her career field-goal percentage was an incredible 63.3 percent.

6. REBECCA LOBO

A two-time All-American at Connecticut, Rebecca Lobo led her team to a 35-0 record and a national championship in 1995. Lobo earned national player of the year honors that year.

7. ANN MEYERS

Ann Meyers received the first athletic scholarship awarded to a woman at UCLA and averaged 17.4 points per game from 1982 to 1986. Meyers was drafted by the Indiana Pacers of the NBA in 1978. Although she didn't make the team, her contributions to basketball were recognized when she was inducted into the Basketball Hall of Fame in 1993.

8. CHAMIQUE HOLDSCLAW

One of the most athletic players in women's basketball, Chamique Holdsclaw led Tennessee to three consecutive women's titles in the late 1990s. Prior to enrolling in Tennessee, she played on four straight high-school state champions in New York.

9. DENISE CURRY

The all-time scoring leader at UCLA with 3,198 points, Denise Curry was a three-time All-American. Curry averaged 28.5 points per game during her senior season in 1981.

10. CAROL MENKEN SCHAUDT

Carol Menken Schaudt averaged 27.7 points per game in her career at Oregon State. During the 1980–81 season, she shot an outstanding 75 percent from the field and scored nearly 30 points per game.

Unsung Heroes

The memory of many early basketball greats has dimmed over the years. These players were some of yesteryear's biggest stars.

1. JOHNNY BECKMAN

All but forgotten today, Johnny Beckman was one of basketball's first major attractions. The 5′9″ Beckman was a prolific scorer, exceptional dribbler, and deadly shooter. He barnstormed around the country playing for teams such as West Hoboken, Union Hill Troys, the Deneri Five of Philadelphia, and Naticoke. In 1926, his contract was purchased by Baltimore of the American Basketball League for a record sum of $10,000.

2. HARRY HOUGH

Harry Hough was generally regarded as the best basketball player of the century's first decade. Only 5′8″, he possessed amazing speed and the ability to dribble around the opposition. He played for many teams on the East Coast and often led his team in scoring.

3. CHRIS STEINMETZ

Basketball's first scoring sensation, Chris Steinmetz, was the first player to rack up more than 1,000 points in a career. Steinmetz starred at the University of Wisconsin in 1905 and 1906. He averaged more than 25 points per game at a time when whole teams rarely scored that many points. As a junior, he notched 462 points, 23 more than the total of all of Wisconsin's opponents. Steinmetz tallied 50 points in a game against Sparta College and his 20 field goals against Beloit remain a school record.

4. CAT THOMPSON

John "Cat" Thompson scored 1,539 points during his three seasons at Montana State, a span in which the Bobcats won 72 games and lost only four. Thompson, the 1929 Helms Foundation Player of the Year, led Montana State to the nation's number-one ranking.

5. VIC HANSON

A three-time All-American at Syracuse, Vic Hanson led his team to the national championship in 1927. That season he was named the Helms Foundation Player of the Year. He set a school scoring record that lasted for 20 years.

6. JOHN SCHOMMER

Although he stood only six feet tall, John Schommer of the University of Chicago was a larger-than-life figure. Schommer led the Western Conference in scoring from 1907 to 1909. He was also a tremendous defensive player and frequently held opposing centers scoreless. He made an 80-foot last-second shot against Pennsylvania to clinch the 1908 national championship for Chicago.

7. **ED WACHTER**

Ed Wachter was an innovator both as a player and as a coach. The best center of his time, he played professionally from 1901 to 1924. When he played for the Troy (New York) Trojans, the team was so dominant that its success ultimately resulted in the collapse of the league. Wachter also coached college basketball for 25 years and helped introduce many elements into the game, such as the fast break and the man-to-man defense.

8. **ELMER OLIPHANT**

Elmer Oliphant played for Purdue and Army during the years 1912 to 1918. Oliphant once helped Purdue beat Illinois with a field goal despite a broken ankle. Another time he made a shot while seated on the court.

9. **BOBBY MCDERMOTT**

Bobby McDermott was one of the best players of the 1930s and 1940s. He led both the American Basketball League and National Basketball League in scoring. He was the MVP of the National Basketball League five consecutive seasons and led the Fort Wayne Pistons to two championships. At the age of 37, he scored 48 points in an exhibition game against the New York Knicks.

10. **STRETCH MURPHY**

Charles "Stretch" Murphy of Purdue was a first-team All-American in 1929 and 1930. The 6'6" player was a giant in his day. He teamed with John Wooden to lead Purdue to a national championship.

Early African-American Stars

Today, African-American athletes dominate college and professional basketball, but for many years they were not permitted to play on teams with white players. In January 1947, the University of Miami was forced to cancel a game with Duquesne scheduled for the Orange Bowl because of a city ordinance that prohibited black athletes from competing with whites. Duquesne had a black player, Chuck Cooper, on the team. A month earlier, the University of Tennessee had refused to play Duquesne even when coach Chick Davies agreed to hold Cooper out of the game. When John Wooden coached Indiana State in the late 1940s, he refused to participate in the NAIA Tournament when they informed him that a black player on his team would not be permitted to play. Mississippi State, a college basketball powerhouse in the late 1950s, did not play in the NCAA tournament for three years because state politicians opposed the school's participation in the integrated tournament. It was not until 1966 that the University of North Carolina offered its first basketball scholarship to a black athlete, Charlie Scott. Even those black athletes who were permitted to play often could not eat their meals or stay in the same hotels as their white teammates. The following men paved the way for the black basketball stars of today.

1. DON BARKSDALE

In 1947, Don Barksdale of UCLA became the first African-American to be named consensus All-American. The following year, the 6'6" forward became the first black athlete to play on a U.S. Olympic team. He played four seasons in the NBA for Baltimore and Boston. In 1953, Barksdale achieved another milestone when he became the first African-American to appear in an NBA All-Star Game. He averaged nearly 14 points per game during the 1952–53 season.

2. CHUCK COOPER

Duquesne All-American Chuck Cooper was the first African-American drafted by the NBA. He was selected by the Boston Celtics in 1950. When Celtics owner Walter Brown was reminded by another owner that Cooper was black, he replied, "I don't give a damn if he's plaid." Cooper played six seasons in the NBA and averaged 6.7 points.

3. TARZAN COOPER

Charles "Tarzan" Cooper was one of the best players of the 1930s. From 1929 to 1939, he played for the all-black New York Rens. During his years with the Rens, the team won 1,303 games and lost only 203, including one stretch of 88 wins in a row. The 6'4" Cooper was considered the best center of his time.

In 1947, Don Barksdale, *right,* of UCLA became the first African American to be named a consensus All-American player.

4. **EARL LLOYD**

Earl "Big Cat" Lloyd holds the distinction of being the first African-American to play in an NBA game. On October 30, 1950, the former West Virginia State star took the court with the Washington Capitols in a game versus Rochester. Lloyd played in the NBA for Washington, Syracuse, and Detroit, retiring in 1960. His best season was 1955, when he averaged 10.2 points for Syracuse.

5. **DOLLY KING**

Dolly King was one of the first black stars in college basketball. He played on the undefeated Long Island University team in 1939. He became the first African-American to play in the National Basketball League, predecessor of the NBA, in the 1946–47 season with Rochester. King also played with the all-black Dayton Rens of the NBL in 1949.

6. **FATS JENKINS**

Clarence "Fats" Jenkins was another star of the famed New York Rens teams of the 1930s. The 5'7" guard was the quickest player of his time. With Jenkins running the club, the Rens won nearly 90 percent of their games between 1932 and 1936.

7. **POP GATES**

Another star with the New York Rens was William "Pop" Gates. The Rens signed Gates to a $125-a-month contract in 1938. He sparked the team to a victory over the Oshkosh All-Stars, the National Basketball League champion, in the World Professional Tournament. Red Holzman, who coached the New York Knicks to NBA championships in 1970 and

1973, called Gates "the greatest player of his day." Gates played with Tri-Cities of the NBL in 1946 and two seasons later became the first black coach with the Dayton Rens.

8. **GEORGE GREGORY**

One of the first African-Americans to star on a white college team was George Gregory. He was an Eastern Conference center with Columbia University in 1928 and 1929. An excellent shooter, he finished fourth in the conference in scoring.

9. **SWEETWATER CLIFTON**

Nat "Sweetwater" Clifton was one of the best-known players of his era. He received his distinctive nickname because of his love for soda pop. Clifton was the first African-American to sign a contract to play in the NBA, inking a deal with the New York Knicks in 1950. Although he did not begin his NBA career until he was 28 years old, Clifton played eight seasons in the league and appeared in the 1957 All-Star Game.

10. **RAY FELIX**

Ray Felix was the first outstanding black center in the NBA. The 6'11" Felix won Rookie of the Year honors when he averaged 17.6 points for Baltimore during the 1953–54 season. That year he became the second African-American to play in the NBA All-Star Game. Felix averaged nearly 11 points a game during his nine-year pro career.

Tall Men

Seven-foot one-inch Wilt Chamberlain was considered a giant when he set NBA scoring records during the early 1960s, but even Wilt the Stilt would have had to look up to these men.

1. SULEIMAN ALI NASHNUSH

Suleiman Ali Nashnush was the tallest player in international basketball history. The eight-footer played for the Libyan national team in 1962.

2. GHEORGHE MURESAN

Skeptics snickered when the Washington Bullets selected 7′7″ Romanian Gheorghe Muresan in the 1993 NBA draft. It was believed that the lumbering Muresan was too slow-footed to play in the NBA. Muresan proved his critics wrong by becoming a solid center with the Bullets, leading the NBA in field-goal percentage in 1996 and 1997.

3. **MANUTE BOL**

There was nothing minute about Manute Bol. The 7′7″ Bol played nine seasons in the NBA, primarily as a defensive specialist. Although he averaged less than three points a game, the former Dinka tribesman blocked more than 2,000 shots during his career.

4. **ARTIS GILMORE**

Artis Gilmore played on a Jacksonville team that met UCLA in the 1970 NCAA championship game. Gilmore was the tallest player on a front line that averaged seven feet in height. The 7′2″ Gilmore played five seasons with the Kentucky Colonels of the ABA. He was billed as being 7′7″ because of his enormous five-inch Afro. Gilmore played in the NBA from 1976 to 1988 and set the league all-time field-goal percentage record, making 59.9 percent of his shots.

5. **SHAWN BRADLEY**

Seven-foot six-inch Shawn Bradley played college basketball at Brigham Young. On December 7, 1990, he set an NCAA record by blocking 14 shots in a game against Eastern Kentucky. Despite playing only one season at Brigham Young (he spent two years as a Mormon missionary), Bradley was the second pick of the 1993 NBA draft. Bradley has averaged more than 10 points a game during his NBA career with Philadelphia, New Jersey, and Dallas.

6. **RALPH SAMPSON**

Ralph Sampson has always been considered something of a disappointment. A three-time college player of the year at

Artis Gilmore's 7'2" height (7'7" with the Afro) put him close to the rim and helped him to make 59.9 percent of his career shots, a NBA record.

Virginia, the 7'4" Sampson was never able to lead the Cavaliers to a national title. Drafted by the Houston Rockets, Sampson became part of the famed "Twin Towers" with Hakeem Olajuwon. Sampson averaged more than 20 points per game during his first two seasons but was soon over-shadowed by his teammate. His point production dropped drastically, and he was traded to Golden State during the 1987–88 season.

7. RIK SMITS

Born in Holland, Rik Smits was the second pick in the 1988 NBA draft, despite having played for tiny Marist College. Standing 7'4", he was one of the best-shooting big men in the NBA. He spent his entire career with the Indiana Pacers and averaged nearly 15 points per game. The "Dunkin' Dutchman" retired following the 2000 season after helping the Pacers to their first appearance in the NBA finals.

8. MARK EATON

Mark Eaton was a part-time player with UCLA before being picked by Utah in the fourth round of the 1982 NBA draft. Once he turned pro, the 7'4" center soon became one of the league's best shot blockers. In 1985, he set an NBA record with 456 blocks and was voted Defensive Player of the Year.

9. TOM BURLESON

Seven-foot four-inch Tom Burleson was a big reason that North Carolina State won the 1974 NCAA championship. That year, the All-American center averaged more than 18 points and 12 rebounds per game. Burleson scored 20 points in the much anticipated semifinal victory over defending champion UCLA. He played seven seasons in the NBA. His best year was 1976, when he averaged 15.6 points per game for the Seattle Super Sonics.

10. **SWEDE HALBROOK**

Swede Halbrook played college basketball at Oregon State. The 7'3" Halbrook was a member of the NBA's Syracuse Nationals from 1960 to 1962.

Small Packages

Basketball is a game that favors tall people, but these players proved that good things can indeed come in small packages.

1. DEBBIE BROCK

Despite being only 4'11", Debbie Brock played on three consecutive AIAW (Association for Intercollegiate Athletics for Women) championship teams at Delta State. An All-American in 1976 and 1977, she scored 22 points in the 1977 national championship game against Louisiana State.

2. ABE SAPERSTEIN

Abe Saperstein founded the Harlem Globetrotters in 1927. During the early years the five-foot Saperstein, nicknamed "Little Caesar," served as the team's only substitute player.

3. MUGGSY BOGUES

Tyrone "Muggsy" Bogues defied the odds by playing in the NBA for more than a dozen years. Only 5'3", Bogues was an All Atlantic Coast Conference selection while playing for Wake Forest in 1987. Picked in the first round of the 1987 draft by the Washington Bullets, Bogues scored more than 6,000 points and dished more than 6,000 assists during his NBA career.

4. BUNNY LEVITT

Five-foot four-inch Harold "Bunny" Levitt was one of the great free-throw shooters of all time. On April 6, 1935, Levitt made 499 consecutive free throws. After missing one, he began another streak of 371.

5. BARNEY SEDRAN

Known as the "Mighty Mite of Basketball," Barney Sedran stood 5′ 4″ and weighed only 110 pounds. Sedran was a star at DeWitt Clinton High School in New York and at the City College of New York. He excelled at every aspect of the game: shooting, passing, and defense. Sedran led Utica to the world professional championship in 1914. That year he scored 34 points in a game despite not having a backboard to bank his shots.

6. SPUD WEBB

Anthony "Spud" Webb played college basketball at North Carolina State. The 5′ 7″, 135-pound Spud shocked the basketball world by winning the 1986 NBA slam dunk competition. Like Muggsy Bogues, Webb showed he could play with big guys and remained in the NBA for a dozen seasons.

7. JOHNNY O'BRIEN

During the 1951–52 season, Johnny O'Brien became the first college player to score more than 1,000 points in a season.

O'Brien played on a Seattle team that included his twin brother, Eddie. The All-American averaged more than 28 points per game during his junior and senior seasons. In January 1952, O'Brien played in an exhibition game against the Harlem Globetrotters. The 5'8" O'Brien was matched in the pivot against the much taller and experienced Goose Tatum. O'Brien dazzled the crowd with a 43-point performance and handed a rare defeat to the Globetrotters. O'Brien was drafted by the NBA Milwaukee Hawks in 1953 but decided to play baseball. He was an infielder in the major leagues from 1953 to 1959.

8. **CALVIN MURPHY**

Calvin Murphy had a talent far greater than his 5'9" height. At Niagara, he was one of the most prolific scorers in college basketball history. The two-time All-American averaged more than 38 points during the 1967–68 season and 33.1 points for his college career. He scored 68 points in a game against Syracuse during his junior year. Murphy played in the NBA from 1970 to 1983, all but one year with the Houston Rockets. His best season was 1977–78 when he averaged 25.6 points. One of the greatest free-throw shooters in NBA history, his career percentage was 89.2. In 1981, Murphy made an amazing 95.8 percent of his free throws. Murphy explained his success by noting that he was the only normal-sized person in the league.

9. **MURRAY WIER**

At 5'9", Murray Wier was the shortest NCAA scoring champion. The University of Iowa star led the nation in 1948 with a 21-point average.

10. **CHET FORTE**

Chet Forte averaged 28.9 points per game for Columbia during the 1956–57 season. His performance earned him the national player of the year award. The 5'9" Forte beat out 7'1" Wilt Chamberlain of Kansas.

Leaning Towers of Pizza

In 2000, the Orlando Magic announced that they had hired a local company to make nutritional fruit smoothies to supplement their players' diets. These players had food for thought.

1. CHARLES BARKLEY

During his college career at Auburn, Charles Barkley's weight ballooned to as much as 300 pounds. Barkley received a number of nicknames making light of his weight. He was "The Crisco Kid," "Boy Gorge," and "The Round Mound of Rebound." He was also nicknamed "The Leaning Tower of Pizza" for his love of the Italian pie. Barkley routinely ate two large pizzas a night. Fans at opposing schools enjoyed ribbing Barkley about his pizza fixation. University of Kentucky fans waved empty pizza boxes and threw them out onto the floor when Barkley was introduced. A Tennessee fan dressed in a Domino's uniform asked to take Barkley's order during a game. At Louisiana State, they actually delivered a pizza to him. When he turned pro Barkley lost 40 pounds. Asked how he did it, Barkley replied that he cut down to six meals a day.

2. **MARVIN BARNES**

Marvin Barnes averaged 24 points per game with the St. Louis Spirits of the ABA from 1974 to 1976. Barnes was as well known for his enormous appetite as for his scoring feats. Prior to a game, he would eat huge meals of cheeseburgers, nachos, steak, potatoes, and anything else edible in the clubhouse.

3. **DENNIS SCOTT**

Georgia Tech star Dennis Scott went on a diet and lost 30 pounds. Duke fans tried to tempt him by showering him with Twinkies, doughnuts, and bagels during a 1990 game.

4. **CHUCK SOLODARE**

NBA official Chuck Solodare was really hearing it from the fans during a 1952 game in Fort Wayne. Near the end of the game, Solodare pulled a raw steak from beneath his shirt and tossed it into the crowd. "Here, you wolves!" he shouted.

5. **FRANK LAYDEN**

Utah Jazz coach Frank Layden let his appetite get the best of him during a March 12, 1985, game against the Lakers at the Los Angeles Forum. Halfway through the fourth quarter of a 123–108 loss, Layden unexpectedly left the bench. He went back to the hotel coffee shop and ordered a BLT sandwich and a bowl of chili.

6. **ADRIAN DANTLEY**

Adrian Dantley was nicknamed "Baby Huey" because of his fondness for eating, but his weight problem didn't stop him from becoming an All-American at Notre Dame and from winning NBA scoring titles with the Utah Jazz in 1981 and 1984. Jazz coach Frank Layden said of Dantley, "He's a piranha. He'll eat you alive."

7. ROBERT PARISH

Robert Parish, who combined with Larry Bird and Kevin McHale to form one of the greatest front courts in professional basketball history, adhered to a vegetarian diet. Together, the trio led the Boston Celtics to three NBA titles during the 1980s. Parish retired in 1997 after playing a record 21 seasons in the NBA.

8. BILL WALTON

Bill Walton was another outstanding center who was a strict vegetarian. Unlike Parish, Walton had trouble staying healthy. During his NBA career, he missed four entire seasons due to injuries.

9. ELMORE MORGENTHALER

At 7' 1", Elmore Morgenthaler was one of the tallest players of the 1940s. He played college basketball for the New Mexico School of Mines. In an exhibition game against Drury College of Missouri, the teams used 12-foot-high baskets, with each field goal counting three points. Morgenthaler played professional basketball with Providence and Philadelphia from 1946 to 1949. Despite his height, he averaged fewer than two points per game. Morgenthaler kept a wad of gum stashed behind his ear, and he popped it into his mouth when he needed a chew.

10. **SHAWN KEMP**

No one has ever doubted Shawn Kemp's ability, but his attitude has been questioned at times. The Portland Trail Blazers forward was fined after missing a practice on December 19, 2000. Kemp said that he had missed the workout because he overslept. His weariness, he explained, was caused by his new diet.

The One and Only

The following are one-of-a-kind basketball feats.

1. CITY COLLEGE OF NEW YORK

City College of New York is the only college ever to win the NCAA and NIT tournaments the same year. CCNY entered the 1950 postseason unranked in the national polls. The unheralded Beavers upset third-ranked Kentucky, then defeated top-ranked Bradley 69–61 in the championship game of the NIT. A week later, CCNY began competition in the NCAA tournament. CCNY defeated second-ranked Ohio State and fifth-ranked North Carolina State to advance to a rematch with the number-one team in the country, Bradley. CCNY once again beat Bradley, 71–68, to claim the NCAA title. Since teams no longer play in both the NCAA and NIT tournaments, it is likely that City College of New York will remain the only team to win both tournaments in the same year.

2. RICK BARRY

Rick Barry is the only player to lead the NCAA, ABA, and NBA in scoring. While playing for the University of Miami during the 1964–65 season, he led the nation in scoring with a 37.4 average. Two years later, Barry led the NBA with a 35.6-point average with the San Francisco Warriors. Barry was the ABA scoring champion with the Oakland Oaks during the 1968–69 season.

3. NATE ARCHIBALD

The only player to lead the NBA in scoring and assists during the same year is Nate Archibald. He averaged 34.0 points and 11.4 assists per game for Kansas City/Omaha during the 1972–73 season.

4. OSCAR ROBERTSON

The triple double is one of basketball's most difficult feats. A player must reach double figures in three statistical categories: points, rebounds, and assists. Oscar Robertson is the only player to accomplish a triple double for an entire season. The "Big O" averaged 30.8 points, 12.5 rebounds, and 11.4 assists per game for the Cincinnati Royals during the 1961–62 campaign.

5. BOB FEERICK

Bob Feerick is the only player in NBA history to lead the league in field-goal and free-throw percentage in the same year. During the 1947–48 season, Feerick, playing for Washington, topped the league with a .340 field-goal percentage and a .788 free-throw percentage. Feerick also led the NBA in free-throw percentage the next season.

6. **TOM GOLA**

Tom Gola is the only player to be the MVP in both the NIT and NCAA tournaments. Gola was named MVP of the NIT in 1952 as he led LaSalle to the title. In 1954, Gola was MVP of the Final Four as LaSalle won its only NCAA title.

7. **TOM THACKER**

Tom Thacker is the only player to be on NCAA, NBA, and ABA championship teams. Thacker was a starting guard on the University of Cincinnati national championship teams of 1961 and 1962. He was also a member of the NBA champion 1968 Boston Celtics and the ABA champion 1970 Indiana Pacers.

8. **CLYDE LOVELLETTE**

The only player to lead the nation in scoring and play on an NCAA championship team in the same year is Clyde Lovellette of the University of Kansas. He averaged 28.4 points per game during the Jayhawks' 1952 championship season.

9. **PETE MARAVICH**

Pete Maravich is the only three-time All-American to have never played in an NCAA tournament. Maravich led the nation in scoring in 1968, 1969, and 1970, but his Louisiana State Tigers did not qualify for the NCAA tourney.

10. **CARL BOULDIN**

Carl Bouldin is the only athlete to lead his team in scoring during the NCAA Final Four and pitch in the major leagues in the same year. Bouldin tallied 37 points to lead the Cincinnati Bearcats in scoring at the 1961 NCAA Final Four, helping them to win their first national championship. Later that year, he pitched in two games for the Washington Senators. Bouldin spent four seasons with Washington and finished his career with a 3-8 record.

Basketball's Strangest Games

If you think you've seen everything at a basketball game, then think again.

1. RHODE ISLAND–MAINE

On February 22, 1948, the heavily favored University of Rhode Island Rams played the University of Maine Black Bears. In order to keep the score close, Maine went into a stall in the second half. Rhode Island coach Frank Keaney sent player Mike Santoro into the game to play "Silent Night" on his harmonica. The officials were not amused and ejected Santoro. Rhode Island players on the bench read comic books as the action on the court ground to a halt. The mockery continued when Rhode Island lined up in a football formation and center Ken Goodwin punted the ball. Once order was restored, Rhode Island won 55–43.

2. MOREHEAD STATE–TENNESSEE TECH

It seemed as though the January 6, 1951, game between Tennessee Tech and Morehead State would never end. The game was played in a high-school gymnasium because the

Tennessee Tech gym was being repaired. The game clock didn't work properly and was noticeably slow. Seventy-seven fouls were called, and the frequent stoppage of action made the contest even longer. The playing time was twice as long as that of a normal game. Morehead State coach Ellis Johnson played the final few minutes after all but three of his players fouled out. By the time the buzzer finally sounded, a dozen players had been disqualified because of fouls. At one point, Coach Johnson went into the stands and ate popcorn with the students. Tennessee Tech won the marathon 90–88.

3. MISSISSIPPI STATE–TENNESSEE

The Mississippi State basketball gymnasium was known as the Tin Can. Opposing teams hated to play in the ill-equipped gym. This was never more true than it was for Tennessee in a 1938 game. Because there were no locker rooms, the teams had to dress at the football stadium a half mile away. Tennessee coach John Mauer was forced to give his halftime pep talk in the bathroom while spectators came in and out to relieve themselves. To make matters worse, the backboard had just been painted. When Tennessee player Wilton Putnam tried to shoot the ball, the wet paint made the ball stick to his hand. On top of it all, Tennessee lost 25–24.

4. KANSAS–KANSAS STATE

In 1934, Kansas and Kansas State played two games with 12-foot baskets. Besides being two feet higher than regulation, the baskets were moved in so that a six-foot section of the court was in play behind the basket. On December 14, Kansas State won 39–35 at Lawrence, Kansas. Four days later, Kansas won the rematch 40–26 at Manhattan, Kansas. The higher baskets contributed to lower scores even though each field goal counted for three points.

5. COLUMBIA-FORDHAM

The three-point rule in college basketball was not adopted until 1986. However, three-point shots were allowed in a February 7, 1945, game between Columbia and Fordham. Any shot beyond the 21-foot line counted for three points, and players also had the option of shooting regular one-point free throws from 15 feet or taking two-point free throws from beyond the 21-foot line. Twenty 3-point shots were made during the game in addition to eight long fouls. Columbia won 73–58.

6. MINNEAPOLIS-FORT WAYNE

On November 22, 1950, Minneapolis and Fort Wayne played a game so boring that it led to a major rule change in the NBA. In those days, there was no shot clock to speed up play. The defending champion Minneapolis Lakers had won 29 games in a row at home. Fort Wayne coach Murray Mendenhall ordered his players to go into a stall. Minneapolis led 13–11 at halftime. In the final quarter, only four points were scored. Larry Foust made a basket with time running out to give the Pistons a 19–18 victory, ending the Lakers' winning streak. Fans were so incensed by the slowdown tactics that they chased the players into the clubhouse. It took 90 minutes before it was safe for the Fort Wayne players to come out. The notorious game led to the installation of a 24-second clock a few years later.

7. BLUEFIELD STATE-BECKLEY

Bluefield State College coach Larkin Rucker devised a trick play that he used to defeat Beckley College. Rucker had guard Don McDowell go to the lobby to get a drink of water. Instead of going to the lobby, McDowell walked around to the other side of the court. Twice he fooled the Beckley defense and made uncontested lay-ups. His baskets made the difference in a 90–86 Bluefield State win.

8. TRIPLE-HEADER

In 1931, a rare college basketball triple-header was played at Madison Square Garden. Fewer than 100 points were scored in the three games combined. Columbia defeated Fordham 20–18 in the opener, which proved to be the highest-scoring game of the day. Manhattan edged New York University 16–14 in the second game. The final contest, in which St. John's defeated City College of New York 17–9, was a real snoozer. Fans booed throughout the game as St. John's players stalled to protect their lead. The next year, the 10-second rule was adopted, making it an infraction not to get the ball over the half-court line in the allotted time.

9. CINCINNATI-BRADLEY

On December 21, 1981, it took Cincinnati 75 minutes to defeat Bradley 75–73 in the longest college game ever played. Doug Schloemer sank an 18-foot jumper with one second left in the seventh overtime to give the Bearcats the victory.

10. UNLV-TEMPLE

Richard Robinson helped the University of Nevada-Las Vegas to upset Temple even though he was not in the game at the time. Temple entered the January 24, 1988, contest undefeated in 14 games. The Owls led 58–54 late in the game when the ball went out of bounds. Robinson, seated on the UNLV bench, batted it to teammate Keith James, who made a three-point basket. The referees did not see Robinson touch the ball. UNLV won 59–58, handing Temple its only loss of the regular season.

Hoop Oddities

S ometimes fact is stranger than fiction.

1. UTAH

In 1944, Utah turned down an invitation to play in the NCAA tournament because the players wanted to see New York City, where the NIT was held. Their season appeared to be over when they lost in the first round of the NIT to Kentucky. Utah got a second chance when Arkansas was forced to withdraw from the NCAA tournament after two players were badly hurt in an automobile accident. Utah replaced the Razorbacks in the tournament and made the most of the opportunity by winning the title.

2. BRADLEY–OKLAHOMA CITY

The NCAA tournament generally is reserved for the best college teams. The 1955 tournament, however, matched Bradley and Oklahoma City, the teams with the two worst records in tournament history. Bradley, with a 7-19 record, defeated 9-17 Oklahoma City 69–55. Bradley also upset Southern

Methodist University before losing to Colorado in the regional finals.

3. LONG ISLAND UNIVERSITY

Long Island University won all 23 of its games in 1939, including the NIT championship. They played all but one of their games in New York, the exception coming against LaSalle in Philadelphia.

4. NORTH ATLANTIC TOURNAMENT

The 1989 North Atlantic Conference tournament was played in front of completely empty stands. Spectators were banned from the arena because of a measles epidemic.

5. EDGERTON PARK ARENA

The NBA's Rochester Royals played their home games in the Edgerton Park Arena from 1948 to 1957. The arena was so small that there was no room behind the baskets. Players driving to the hoop risked slamming into the gymnasium wall. Attendants held open doors so that players would literally exit the building when they were unable to stop their momentum. Occasionally, a player would land in a snow drift or crash into a late-arriving fan.

6. SNOW HALL

Snow Hall, an early gymnasium at the University of Kansas, had ceilings that were only 11 feet high. Shots with high trajectories frequently hit the ceiling. The school devised an unusual solution, lowering the floor five feet. Players had to climb down ladders to reach the court.

7. **POTSDAM–PLATTSBURGH**

There was nothing normal about the 1904 game between Potsdam Normal College of New York and Plattsburgh Normal College. Potsdam shut out Plattsburgh 123–0.

8. **KANSAS STATE**

During the 1905 season, Kansas State University shut out Salina College 24–0, Haskell College 60–0, and Kansas Normal 10–0. That same season, Kansas State was defeated by the University of Kansas 28–0.

9. **RIO GRANDE COLLEGE**

Alumni of Rio Grande College in Ohio played a game that lasted 125 hours. Each team had 15 players, and five-man squads played in four-hour rotations. The White team defeated the Red 10,752–10,734.

10. **QUENEMO HIGH SCHOOL**

In 1977, Quenemo High School in Kansas had one of the worst teams in memory. With a student body of only 40 and no player taller than 5'5", the girls' team usually came out on the short end of the score. In January 1977, they lost to LeRoy High School 83–1. In a game against Malvern High, five Quenemo players fouled out, leaving only one player on the court. The Malvern coach, in a sportsmanlike gesture, removed a player each time a Quenemo player fouled out. Even with the help, Quenemo High suffered yet another defeat.

You Can Look It Up

These basketball records and events are almost unbelievable.

1. G. KINNEY

Basketball in its infancy was a very low-scoring game. Consider G. Kinney of New York University. He won the Eastern Intercollegiate scoring title despite tallying only 31 points all season.

2. LEROY EDWARDS

The National Basketball League was the predecessor of the NBA. Oshkosh's Leroy Edwards won the league's first scoring title in 1940 with a measly 9.0-point average.

3. TED ST. MARTIN

Without a doubt, the most accurate free-throw shooter in basketball history was Ted St. Martin of Jacksonville, Florida. On February 28, 1975, St. Martin made an incredible 1,704 consecutive free throws. St. Martin later bettered his own record by making 2,036 free throws.

4. FRED NEWMAN

On February 5, 1978, Fred Newman made 88 consecutive free throws at the Central YMCA in San Jose, California. What made the feat so amazing is that he was blindfolded at the time.

5. BONES MCKINNEY

Horace "Bones" McKinney was one of pro basketball's free spirits. McKinney averaged 9.4 points per game during his NBA career, which lasted from 1946 to 1952. While playing for the Washington Capitols in a blowout victory over the New York Knicks, McKinney turned his back to the basket and took a free throw over his head. He missed the shot. On another occasion, he bowed to the crowd before making a free throw.

6. BOBBY ANET

During the championship game of the 1939 NCAA tournament, Oregon's Bobby Anet dove for a loose ball and knocked over the trophy, breaking it in half. After Oregon defeated Ohio State 46–32, the team took home the trophy in two pieces.

7. TONY LAVELLI

An All-American at Yale, Tony Lavelli played with the Boston Celtics during the 1949–50 season. Not only did Lavelli average nearly nine points per game, he also entertained the Boston Garden crowds at halftime by playing the accordion.

8. **TOM KING**

Tom King played guard for the Detroit Falcons during the 1946–47 season, averaging 5.1 points per game in what proved to be his only year as a professional. King also served as the team's publicist. After each game, he could be seen typing press statements while still in uniform.

9. **RUSSELL THOMPSON**

In a January 30, 1971, game against Florence State University, Russell Thompson of Birmingham Southern State College scored 25 points in a 55–46 victory. Incredibly, all 25 of Thompson's points came on free throws.

10. **MIKE PENBERTHY**

One of the NBA's most unbelievable success stories belongs to Los Angeles Lakers' guard Mike Penberthy. In 2000, the 26-year-old rookie made the roster of the defending NBA champion Lakers. In 1997, Penberthy had graduated from the Master's College (enrollment 850) with a degree in Bible exposition. Cut by the Indiana Pacers, he was then released by the Quad City Thunder of the Continental Basketball Association after only four games. In 1998, he had made eight dollars an hour while working for the United Parcel Service.

Believe It or Not

It's all true.

1. OTIS SMITH

Jacksonville University guard Otis Smith had never fouled out of a game until a March 2, 1984, matchup against Old Dominion University. With less than three minutes remaining, Smith picked up his fifth foul. Not realizing he had fouled out, he stayed in the game. He played for 90 more seconds and scored another basket before officials realized their mistake and removed him. Old Dominion won 79–68.

2. DOUG MOE

Denver Nuggets coach Doug Moe was disgusted with his players' lack of defensive play in a 156–116 loss to the Portland Trail Blazers on November 22, 1983. The Nuggets trailed 146–116 with a minute to go when Moe ordered his players to stop defending Portland players. As a result, Portland made five uncontested lay-ups. Moe was fined $5,000 and suspended two games for his behavior.

3. **JAMES NAISMITH**

James Naismith invented basketball in 1891 more as a form of exercise than as a competitive game. In 1900, he became the basketball coach at Kansas. In his first game against Nebraska, Naismith's Jayhawks were embarrassed 48–8. Naismith's record during his 12 seasons at Kansas was 55 wins and 60 loses, giving him the dubious distinction of being the only coach in Kansas basketball history to compile a losing record.

4. **HAROLD FOSTER**

Harold Foster coached at the University of Wisconsin from 1935 to 1959. In 1941, Foster's Badgers won the NCAA title. Foster compiled a career mark of 265 wins and 267 losses. Despite his losing record, he was elected to the Basketball Hall of Fame in 1964.

5. **JIM BREWER**

Minnesota's Jim Brewer won the Big Ten Conference's MVP award in 1972. The honor came as a surprise since Brewer had not been selected to the first or second All-Conference team.

6. **PAUL ARIZIN**

Paul Arizin did not try out for his high-school team until his senior year and was not even good enough to make the squad. After graduation, he played on church and independent teams in the city—as many as seven different teams at once. He perfected his skills, and by the time he enrolled at Villanova, he was an outstanding player. Arizin scored 85 points in a game and led the nation in scoring during the 1949–50 season. He also led the NBA in scoring in 1952 and 1957.

7. **BILL RUSSELL**

In high school, Bill Russell was an uncoordinated 130-pound benchwarmer at McClymonds in Oakland. He received only one scholarship offer, from the University of San Francisco. In college, he grew to 6'9" and developed into an All-American player. He led San Francisco to two NCAA titles, and his arrival in Boston marked the beginning of the Celtics dynasty.

8. **HAL LEAR**

Bill Russell led San Francisco to the NCAA title in 1956. Surprisingly, Russell was not the Final Four MVP. That honor belonged to Temple's Hal Lear, who averaged 32 points, including a 48-point outburst against Southern Methodist University in the consolation game.

9. **JOHN WOODEN**

John Wooden learned how to play basketball by stuffing rags into his mother's hose and shooting them into a tomato basket attached to the family barn. Wooden became a three-time All-American at Purdue University and a coaching legend at UCLA.

10. **TEXAS A&M**

Texas A&M met North Carolina in the second round of the 1980 NCAA tournament. The teams were tied 53–53 at the end of regulation. Both teams went scoreless in the overtime. In the second overtime, Texas A&M exploded for a record 25 overtime points in a 78–61 victory.

Draft Follies

Each year, the NBA teams select the top college and eligible high-school players in the draft. For every successful draft pick such as Michael Jordan and Vince Carter, there are draft disappointments such as Joe Barry Carroll and Benoit Benjamin.

1. BEN SWAIN

The Boston Celtics built their dynasty with a series of excellent draft choices. Between 1953 and 1962, the Celtics drafted Frank Ramsey, Jim Loscutoff, Bill Russell, Sam Jones, Tom Sanders, and John Havlicek in the first round. One of their draft busts was Ben Swain, their first-round pick in the 1958 draft. The 6′8″ forward from Texas Southern averaged 4.6 points per game in his only year in the NBA.

2. SIHUGO GREEN

The Rochester Royals had the first pick of the 1956 NBA draft. University of San Francisco center Bill Russell was a no-brainer choice. Russell had led his team to two consecutive

NCAA titles. Rochester, apparently unwilling to pay the large salary Russell would demand, instead chose Duquesne guard Sihugo Green. The Boston Celtics made a trade with the St. Louis Hawks for the right to pick Russell. He led the Celtics to 11 NBA championships. Green played in six different cities in nine years. A solid but not spectacular performer, he averaged nine points per game. He finished his career with Russell and the Celtics in 1966.

3. **SAM BOWIE**

The 1984 NBA draft was filled with exceptional talent. The Houston Rockets selected University of Houston center Hakeem Olajuwon with the first pick of the draft. Olajuwon justified the selection by leading the Rockets to two NBA championships. The Portland Trail Blazers passed over Michael Jordan with the second pick, instead selecting Kentucky's seven-foot center, Sam Bowie. Bowie averaged 10 points a game as a rookie in Portland. Injury-prone, he never became a star in the NBA. With the third pick, the Chicago Bulls selected North Carolina's Jordan, who led the Bulls to six NBA titles and retired with the highest scoring average in league history. (Other 1984 first-round picks included Charles Barkley and John Stockton.)

4. **LARUE MARTIN**

The Portland Trail Blazers made another blunder when they selected Loyola of Chicago center Larue Martin with the first pick of the 1972 draft. Martin lasted four seasons in the NBA and averaged five points per game.

5. **RALPH POLSON**

The New York Knicks made some questionable first-round picks in the 1950s. In 1952, the Knicks selected Ralph Polson of Whitworth College. Polson averaged 3.9 points per game in his only pro season.

6. **EUGENE SHORT**

Eugene Short had a terrible name for a basketball player. The 6′7″ player was the New York Knicks' first-round pick in 1975 out of Jackson State. His NBA career was short, as he averaged 2.5 points per game in his only season.

7. **AL HENRY**

In 1970, the Philadelphia 76ers selected Al "The Tree" Henry with their top pick. Henry, a 6′9″, 190-pound forward from the University of Wisconsin, scored only 194 points during his two years in the NBA.

8. **WAYNE YATES**

The Los Angeles Lakers selected Elgin Baylor in the first round of the 1958 draft and two years later selected Jerry West. In 1961, they thought they had another gem when they picked Wayne Yates of Memphis State, but Yates averaged less than two points per game in his only season in Los Angeles.

9. **LEO RAUTINS**

The year before they drafted Charles Barkley, the Philadelphia 76ers selected Syracuse's Leo Rautins with their first pick in the 1983 draft. Rautins scored only 48 points in two seasons in the NBA.

10. **BRENDAN McCANN**

The New York Knicks squandered their first-round draft pick in 1957 on St. Bonaventure's Brendan McCann. The guard scored only 75 points during his three seasons in New York.

Dumb Decisions

D umb decisions have lost games, hurt careers, and even changed the course of basketball history.

1. RED AUERBACH

Before he coached the Boston Celtics, Arnold "Red" Auerbach was coach of the NBA's Tri-Cities Blackhawks. The Tri-Cities represented Davenport, Iowa, and Rock Island and Moline, Illinois. Auerbach coached the Hawks during the 1949–50 season. The Hawks let Auerbach go after a dispute, and he immediately signed with the Boston Celtics. Auerbach led the Celtics to 11 NBA championships in 16 seasons. If the Hawks had re-signed Auerbach, they might have had their own dynasty in St. Louis, where they moved in 1955.

2. BOB COUSY

Red Auerbach built the Boston Celtics into pro basketball's greatest team through a series of brilliant draft choices. In 1950, however, he made a bad pick that nearly cost the Celtics one of their greatest stars. Bob Cousy had been an All-American guard at Holy Cross. It seemed a natural move for Boston to select their local hero. Auerbach instead drafted

The Celtics passed up Bob Cousy, *number 14,* in the draft, but Cousy ended up playing for the Celtics his rookie year after his team, the Chicago Stags, folded. Cousy went on to make the All-NBA First Team 10 years straight, was the league's most valuable player in 1957, and led the league in assists eight times.

Bowling Green's 6'11" center, Charlie Share. When asked why he had not selected Cousy, Auerbach replied, "Little men are a dime a dozen. I'm supposed to win, not go after local yokels." Cousy was drafted by Auerbach's former team, the Tri-Cities Blackhawks. The Blackhawks then traded Cousy to the Chicago Stags. The Chicago franchise folded, and Cousy became part of a dispersal draft with Chicago players Max Zaslofsky and Andy Phillip. Zaslofsky and Phillip were selected by other teams, and Cousy went to Boston by default. Share, who was traded to Ft. Wayne, never played a game with Boston. He spent nine seasons with the Hawks, averaging 8.3 points per game. Cousy was named to the All-NBA First Team for 10 consecutive years. He topped the league in assists eight consecutive years, and his playmaking skills led the Celtics to six NBA championships. He was voted the league's MVP in 1957.

3. JOHN WOODEN

At the beginning of his career, John Wooden coached at Indiana State. In 1949, he was offered the coaching job at the University of Minnesota. Wooden informed them that he would accept the position if he were permitted to bring along one of his assistant coaches. When Minnesota balked, Wooden took the coaching job at UCLA. The Bruins won 10 NCAA titles during the Wooden years, while Minnesota has yet to win a national championship.

4. KORY HALLAS

Eastern Michigan guard Kory Hallas actually lost a game against Ball State by making a basket. Eastern Michigan trailed Ball State in the closing seconds of a Mid-American Conference tournament game on March 11, 1989. Hallas

UCLA

John Wooden is arguably the greatest coach in college basketball history. His UCLA teams won 10 NCAA championships, giving him far more titles than any other coach. During his tenure at UCLA, he mentored two of the greatest players in the history of the sport, Lew Alcindor and Bill Walton.

drove to the basket and made what he thought was a game-tying lay-up at the buzzer. He knew something was wrong when he noticed his teammates were not joining in the celebration. When Hallas looked at the scoreboard, he realized that his team had been three points down and that his lay-up had still left them a point behind. If he had attempted a three-point shot, he might have tied the game. Instead, Eastern Michigan lost 77–76 and was eliminated from the tournament.

5. GALE CATLETT

West Virginia and Temple were tied 66–66 with just over three minutes remaining on January 11, 1990. During a time-out, West Virginia coach Gale Catlett was so involved in giving his team defensive instructions that he did not notice when the warning horn sounded. Temple's Mark Macon inbounded the ball and drove the length of the court for an uncontested lay-up while the Mountaineer players watched helplessly. Temple won the game 73–69.

6. MITCH BUONAGURO

Fairfield coach Mitch Buonaguro was overjoyed when Harold Brantley made a basket to give his team a 60–59 lead with two seconds remaining in a 1988 game against St. Peters. In his excitement, the coach ran onto the court to embrace Brantley. The officials assessed Buonaguro a technical foul for leaving the bench. St. Peters made the foul shots and went on to a 63–60 victory.

7. BILL FRIEDER

Prior to the 1989 NCAA tournament, Michigan coach Bill Frieder announced that he had accepted the coaching position at Arizona State. Outraged, the Michigan athletic director fired Frieder and named Steve Fisher the new Wolverine coach. Fisher made the most of the opportunity, leading Michigan to its first NCAA title. Frieder was never able to coach Arizona State to a Final Four appearance, while Michigan played in the title games in 1992 and 1993.

8. CHRIS WEBBER

Michigan star Chris Webber made a costly decision in the closing seconds of the 1993 championship game against North Carolina. Michigan trailed 73–71 with 11 seconds remaining when Webber asked for a time-out. Unfortunately, the Wolverines were out of time-outs, and Michigan was assessed a technical foul. Denied a chance for a last-second shot, Michigan lost 77–71.

9. FRED BROWN

Georgetown trailed North Carolina 63–62 with time running out in the 1982 NCAA championship game. Georgetown's Fred Brown brought the ball up the court. Without looking, he made a cross-court pass to what he thought was his teammate, Eric Smith. Instead, he threw the ball right to North Carolina's James Worthy. The Tar Heels held on to a 63–62 victory.

10. JAMES WORTHY

James Worthy had his own embarrassing moment two years later while playing for the Los Angeles Lakers. In the second game of the 1984 NBA Finals, the Lakers led the Boston Celtics 113–111 with 18 seconds remaining. If the Lakers had been able to run the clock out, they would have opened up a commanding 2-0 advantage in the series.

Worthy threw a lazy pass toward teammate Byron Scott. Boston's Gerald Henderson intercepted it and dribbled the length of the court for a game-tying lay-up. Boston won the game 124–121 and went on to win the series four games to three.

Moments They Would Rather Forget

Here are some of basketball's most embarrassing moments.

1. DICK GARRISON

Little-used Ohio University freshman Dick Garrison was surprised when his coach asked him to enter a game in 1953. Garrison removed his sweatpants and was about to take the court when he realized he had forgotten to put on his shorts. The embarrassed Garrison covered himself and ran to the locker room.

2. RICK BARRY

The San Francisco Warriors led the St. Louis Hawks three games to two in the 1967 Western Division playoffs. On a radio program, Warriors player Rick Barry, the league's leading scorer, said that Hawks' fans were for the birds. The St. Louis fans did not appreciate Barry's comments and pelted him with eggs, tomatoes, hot dogs, and Snickers bars. With three minutes left in the game, Barry went up for a rebound. In the battle for the ball, his shorts were ripped off. Barry ran

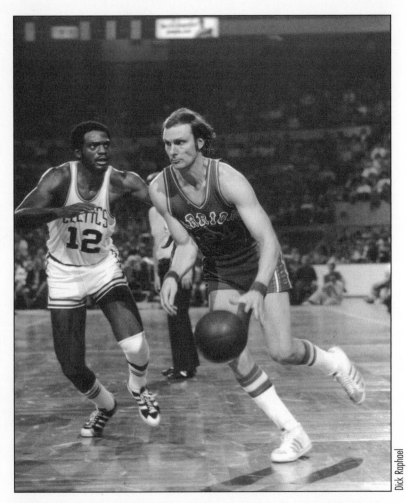

San Francisco Warrior Rick Barry, *right,* was pelted by eggs, tomatoes, hot dogs, and Snickers bars during a 1967 playoff game against the St. Louis Hawks. He had angered the St. Louis fans with some harsh comments during a radio interview.

Dick Raphael

to the locker room for a new pair, and he got the last laugh as he scored 41 points in a 112–107 Warriors' victory.

3. SCOTT THOMPSON

During a 1988 game against Texas A&M, Rice University coach Scott Thompson threw his clipboard in a moment of anger. He then discovered that he'd split his pants. Thompson wrapped his sportscoat around his waist so he could get off the bench.

4. ENGLEWOOD CLIFFS COLLEGE

Englewood Cliffs College, a junior college in New Jersey, suffered a humiliating defeat on January 20, 1974. They lost to Essex County Community College 210–67. The 143-point difference set a record for college basketball futility. Shortly after the debacle, Englewood Cliffs gave up basketball.

5. TERRY HOWARD

The 1975 NCAA tournament was Coach John Wooden's last at UCLA. In the semifinal game against Louisville, the Bruins trailed 74–73 with 20 seconds remaining in overtime. Louisville's best foul shooter, Terry Howard, went to the line, shooting a one-and-one. Howard had not missed a foul shot all season, converting all 28 free-throw attempts. If he made both free throws, Louisville would almost certainly win the game. But Howard missed the first shot, and UCLA escaped with a 75–74 victory. UCLA defeated Kentucky 92–85 in the championship to give Wooden his tenth and final NCAA title.

6. ELMORE SMITH

Seven-foot Elmore Smith helped lead Kentucky State to the 1970 NAIA championship, but Smith did have one game he would rather forget. In a 116–98 defeat against Eastern Michigan, Smith set a record when officials whistled him for 12 goaltending calls.

7. DON LOFGRAN

Don Lofgran was the 1949 NIT MVP, despite tipping in a basket for the opposing team. The University of San Francisco center accidentally scored a basket for Loyola of Chicago in the championship. Luckily for Lofgran, the basket did not cost San Francisco the game. He scored 20 points for his own team as San Francisco prevailed 48–47.

8. CHARLES BARKLEY

Charles Barkley of the Philadelphia 76ers had an off night in a 111–85 loss to the Los Angeles Lakers on January 6, 1987. Three times Barkley dunked the ball, only to have it hit his head and bounce out of the basket.

9. DON KESSINGER

Mississippi's Don Kessinger was one of the best shooters in college basketball, but you wouldn't know it from his performance in a loss against Kentucky on February 8, 1964. Kessinger made only one of 19 shots.

10. BRENT MUSBURGER

During the broadcast of a 1976 Bulls game, announcer Brent Musburger informed fans that Chicago forward Bob Love was the brother of Mike Love of the Beach Boys. In fact, they were not related at all. Bob Love was African-American while Mike Love was Caucasian. Musburger had confused Bob Love with another player, Stan Love, who was indeed Mike Love's brother.

Air Balls

A fifty-percent shooter in the NBA is a great shot. The following players were some of the poorest shooters in NBA history.

1. FRED DIUTE

During his rookie season with the Milwaukee Hawks, Fred Diute made only two of his 21 field-goal attempts. His anemic .095 field-goal percentage may have been the reason his NBA career lasted only seven games.

2. HOWARD MCCARTY

Howard McCarty averaged 1.1 points per game during the 1946–47 season with Detroit. McCarty made only 10 baskets all year, and his .122 field-goal percentage is one of the lowest in league history. Incredibly, his free-throw percentage of .100 was even worse.

3. JOSEPH MULLANEY

Bob Cousy was not the first guard from Holy Cross who played for the Boston Celtics. Joseph Mullaney averaged less than a point a game for the 1949 Celtics. In 37 games, Mullaney made only nine shots, and his field-goal percentage was a dreadful .129.

4. JOHN MCCONATHY

John McConathy averaged one point a game for the Milwaukee Hawks in 1951. Two reasons for his lack of scoring were his .138 field-goal and .429 free-throw percentages.

5. DANIEL KRAUS

Guard Daniel Kraus made only 14.3 percent of his field-goal attempts during the 1948–49 season with Baltimore. He also missed more than half of his free throws.

6. ROBERT FITZGERALD

Robert Fitzgerald played in the NBA for Toronto, New York, and Rochester from 1946 to 1949. During his career, he made 76 of his 391 shots for a .194 field-goal percentage.

7. OSCAR DILLE

Oscar Dille was never mistaken for Oscar Robertson. Dille played for Detroit during the 1946–47 season. He made 111 of 563 shots for a .197 field-goal percentage.

8. HERSCHEL BALTIMORE

Herschel Baltimore averaged two points per game for St. Louis during the 1946–47 season. He shot .202 from the field and .464 from the free-throw line.

9. **ALBERT NEGRATTI**

Seton Hall graduate Albert Negratti made 13 of 69 shots for Washington during the 1946–47 season. His field-goal percentage for his NBA career was .188

10. **WHITEY SCHARNUS**

Whitey Scharnus played for Cleveland and Providence from 1946 to 1949. He averaged two points per game, and his field-goal percentage was .199.

Free-Throw Woes

Because the shooter is unguarded, free-throw percentages are usually much higher than field-goal percentages. Bill Sharman and Rick Barry converted approximately 90 percent of their free-throw attempts. The following players, however, had their difficulties at the free-throw line.

1. CITY COLLEGE OF NEW YORK

In 1911, the City College of New York defeated Renssalaer Polytechnic Institute 20–5. CCNY won the game despite missing all 15 of its free-throw attempts.

2. OLDEN POLYNICE

Olden Polynice made 63.9 percent of his free throws during his rookie season with the Seattle Super Sonics in 1987. Over the years, his free-throw shooting got progressively worse. His free-throw percentages for the 1998 and 1999 seasons were .309 and .311.

3. CHRIS DUDLEY

Chris Dudley earned a reputation as being one of the most inept free-throw shooters in the NBA. The 6'11" center had one of his worst games on April 14, 1990, as his New Jersey Nets lost to the Indiana Pacers 124–113. Dudley missed 17 of 18 free-throw attempts. At one point, he missed 13 consecutive free throws. It was so bad that referee Dick Bavetta patted Dudley on the back in encouragement. In 1990, Dudley made only 31.9 percent of his free throws.

4. ERIC MONTROSS

At the University of North Carolina, center Eric Montross made more than 62 percent of his free throws. As an NBA rookie with the Boston Celtics in 1994, Montross's free-throw percentage was a respectable .635. The next season, his free-throw percentage slipped to .376. The following season, Montross averaged only one free throw made for every three he attempted.

5. ADONAL FOYLE

Adonal Foyle is one of the few players whose field-goal percentage is higher than his free-throw percentage. At Colgate University from 1994 to 1997, Foyle shot 54.7 percent from the floor and 49.1 percent from the foul line. During the 1999–00 season with the Golden State Warriors, Foyle made more than half of his field-goal attempts but less than 38 percent of his free throws.

6. GARFIELD SMITH

Garfield Smith played only two seasons in the NBA, but he is still remembered for his inability to make free throws. He converted less than one of every three free throws in his pro career. During the 1971–72 season with Boston, Smith's free-throw percentage was a dismal .194. On November 17, 1971, Smith's futility reached an absurd level in a 140–121 Celtics victory over the Phoenix Suns. Smith stepped to the free-throw line in a three-shots-to-make-two bonus situation. Smith not only missed all three free throws, but all three were air balls.

7. **VIN BAKER**

All-Star forward Vin Baker had a free-throw lapse during the 1998–99 season with the Seattle Super Sonics. For much of the season, Baker's free-throw percentage was less than 20 percent. His touch eventually returned, and he finished the season with a .450 free-throw percentage. By the next year, his percentage had risen to .682.

8. **SHAQUILLE O'NEAL**

During the 1999–00 season, Los Angeles Lakers' center Shaquille O'Neal led the NBA in scoring and was the league's MVP. O'Neal's only weakness was his poor foul-shooting. In the first game of the 2000 Western Conference finals, the Portland Trail Blazers decided to foul O'Neal repeatedly, using the "Hack a Shaq" strategy in the fourth quarter. O'Neal was fouled on 12 consecutive possessions and shot 25 free throws in the final quarter. For the game, he made 13 of 27 free throws. Despite his poor performance at the line, O'Neal scored 41 points as the Lakers defeated the Trail Blazers 109–94. Los Angeles went on to defeat Portland in the series and capped off a championship season with a victory over the Indiana Pacers in the NBA finals.

9. **WILT CHAMBERLAIN**

Wilt Chamberlain was the most-feared scorer in NBA history, but he never perfected his free-throw technique. He tried numerous styles, from leaping at the basket to shooting underhanded. He set an NBA record for futility when he missed 22 free throws during a game against Seattle on December 1, 1967. For the season, he led the league with a .595 field-goal percentage, but he shot only 38 percent from the foul line.

10. **STEVEN LINGENFELTER**

Steven Lingenfelter played in the NBA briefly with Washington and Seattle from 1982 to 1984. In the 10 games in which he appeared, Lingenfelter made five of seven field goals for an impressive .714 percentage. By contrast, he missed all six of his free-throw attempts.

The Offense Rests

The Duke–North Carolina rivalry has produced some of college basketball's most memorable games. In the 1966 Atlantic Coast Conference tournament, Duke defeated North Carolina 21–20. Duke had led 7–5 at halftime. Thirteen years later, the two teams combined for only seven points in a half. Here are some of the lowest-scoring games in basketball history.

1. ST. MICHAELS–SMITH

During the 1951–52 season, two Massachusetts high schools, St. Michaels and Smith, played one of the lowest-scoring games on record. John Sullivan made the game's only basket in the fourth quarter to give St. Michaels a 2–0 victory.

2. STANFORD–CALIFORNIA

In April 1896, Stanford and California played the first women's intercollegiate basketball game. There were nine players on each side. Seven hundred spectators, all of them women, watched the historic game. Men were not permitted for fear the sight of women in bloomers might be provocative. As it turned out, the game offered very little excitement. Stanford won 2–1.

3. TENNESSEE–TEMPLE

On December 15, 1973, Tennessee and Temple played one of the lowest-scoring games in modern basketball history. Tennessee won 11–6. The Volunteers' Len Kosmalski was the game's high scorer with five points. Tennessee star Eric Grunfeld was held to only two points. After scoring five points in the first half, Temple scored only one point in the second half.

4. FORT WAYNE–MINNEAPOLIS

The lowest-scoring game in NBA history occurred on November 22, 1950. The Fort Wayne Pistons edged the Minneapolis Lakers 19–18. The game was so boring that it eventually led to the installation of the 24-second clock to speed up play.

5. MISSOURI–KANSAS

In 1932, Missouri defeated Kansas 26–22 in a game nearly devoid of offense. During the first half, Missouri kept all its players on one side of the court, and Kansas remained on the other side of the midcourt line. Most of the players sat down while one player held the ball. This travesty of a game was one of the reasons the 10-second rule was adopted the next season.

6. NEW ORLEANS-SOUTH ALABAMA

In 1978, Nate Mills hit a jumper in the closing seconds to give New Orleans a 22–20 victory over South Alabama in the championship game of the Sun Belt tournament. The next year, the Sun Belt became the first conference to use the 45-second shot clock.

7. UCLA-USC

The UCLA–USC rivalry hit a low point in a 1932 game. UCLA defeated Southern California 19–17. USC held the ball for the last 15 minutes of the first half. At one point, a Southern Cal player read a newspaper while fans threw peanuts onto the court. The game was so dead that the UCLA band played taps.

8. KENTUCKY-CINCINNATI

Kentucky and Cincinnati boast two of college basketball's most successful programs. However, Cincinnati had the worst team in school history during the 1983–84 season. The Bearcats won 3 and lost 25. Their most humiliating loss came to Kentucky on December 20, 1983. The outmanned Bearcats slowed down the action in an attempt to keep the score close. The Wildcats won the game 24–11.

9. PENN STATE-PITTSBURGH

In 1952, Penn State defeated Pittsburgh 24–9 in a contest known as the "Freeze Game." The low score was the result of a stall performed by the underdog Panthers.

10. NORTH CAROLINA STATE-DUKE

Interstate rivals North Carolina State and Duke met in the semifinal game of the 1968 Atlantic Coast Conference tournament. The underdog Wolfpack won the game 12–10.

Blown Leads

These teams blew seemingly insurmountable leads.

1. TULANE

Duke staged one of the greatest comebacks in college basketball history during a 1950 game against Tulane. With two minutes remaining in the first half, Tulane led Duke 54–22. Duke trailed 56–29 at halftime. Led by All-American Dick Groat, the Blue Devils staged an amazing comeback, winning 74–72.

2. LOUISIANA STATE

Kentucky seemed hopelessly beaten when they trailed Louisiana 68–37 with 15:30 remaining in a 1994 game, but the Wildcats unleashed a furious second-half comeback to win 99–95. The 31-point deficit was the largest ever overcome by a road team.

3. BRADLEY UNIVERSITY

Bradley appeared to be on its way to routing New Mexico State in a 1977 game. After six minutes, Bradley held a 28–0 lead. New Mexico State chipped away at the deficit, finally taking the lead with just over three minutes left in the game. New Mexico ended up stunning Bradley 117–109.

4. SHASTA COLLEGE

How can a team blow an 18-point lead in 77 seconds? Ask Shasta College of California. Shasta led Butte Community College by 26 points in the first half of a 1990 game. Shasta still led by 18 points with 1:17 remaining. Incredibly, Butte took advantage of a series of Shasta turnovers and missed shots, tying the game in regulation. In overtime, Shasta opened up an 11-point lead with less than two minutes and once again blew it. Butte prevailed 116–115 in double overtime.

5. SOUTH CAROLINA

South Carolina lost a 14-point lead with a minute to go in a game against Louisville on February 20, 1988. At that point, a fight broke out between the two teams. When order was restored, South Carolina was assessed three technical fouls. Louisville rallied and tied the game on a 30-foot jump shot by Craig Hawley at the buzzer. Louisville went on to win 98–88 in overtime.

6. MILWAUKEE BUCKS

One of the most stunning comebacks in NBA history occurred in a November 18, 1972, game between the Milwaukee Bucks and New York Knicks played at Madison Square Garden. The Bucks led New York 86–68 with 5:50 remaining in the fourth quarter. The Knicks scored the final 19 points of the game for a miracle 87–86 victory.

7. UNIVERSITY OF CINCINNATI

The 1963 NCAA championship game matched the two-time defending national champion Cincinnati Bearcats against the Loyola University (Chicago) Ramblers. The Bearcats led the nation in defense, while Loyola led in offense. It looked as though Cincinnati would win its third consecutive title as the team opened up a 15-point lead with 14 minutes remaining. Cincinnati tried a slowdown to protect the lead, but the strategy backfired. Vic Rouse tipped in the winning basket at the buzzer to give Loyola a 60–58 overtime victory.

8. FLORIDA STATE

Florida State led North Carolina 73–54 with 8:50 to go in a game played on January 27, 1993. The Tar Heels uncorked a furious rally and pulled away to a 82–77 comeback win.

9. PRINCETON

Princeton and Michigan played in the 1965 Holiday Festival in New York. The game featured a matchup of two of college's best players, Princeton's Bill Bradley and Michigan's Cazzie Russell. Bradley scored 41 points but fouled out of the game with 4:37 remaining and Princeton leading by 12 points. Russell scored 27 points and led Michigan to an 80–78 comeback win.

10. WAKE FOREST

Wake Forest led North Carolina 41–23 with 17 minutes remaining in a game played on January 27, 1996. North Carolina rallied for a 65–59 win.

Ultimate Upsets

In basketball, nothing is certain.

1. NEW JERSEY REDS

The Harlem Globetrotters carried a 2,495-game winning streak into a January 5, 1971, contest against the New Jersey Reds. New Jersey ended the record streak with a 100–99 victory. The Globetrotters had not lost a game since 1962.

2. GEORGIA TECH

Kentucky set a college record by winning 129 consecutive games at home. The streak ended on January 8, 1955, against Georgia Tech. The Yellow Jackets were an unlikely prospect to upset top-ranked Kentucky. Georgia Tech had struggled to a 2-22 record the previous year and had just lost to tiny Sewanee College. Joe Helms's jump shot with 11 seconds remaining gave Georgia Tech a shocking 59–58 victory. Later in the season, Georgia Tech upset Kentucky again, 65–59.

3. NEBRASKA

In February 1958, Kansas crushed Nebraska 102–46, the worst loss in Cornhusker basketball history. Two weeks later, Nebraska upset the second-ranked Jayhawks 43–41. In their next game, Nebraska upset top-ranked Kansas State. Despite beating the two top-ranked teams in the country, Nebraska finished the season with a 10–11 record.

4. CHAMINADE

Number-one-ranked Virginia was expected to easily defeat unheralded Chaminade College in their 1982 game. Virginia was led by 7'4" center Ralph Sampson, the nation's best player. Chaminade center Tony Randolph scored 19 points and held Sampson to 12 as Chaminade pulled off the upset, 77–72.

5. NORTHWESTERN

Michigan State, led by Magic Johnson, won the NCAA title in 1979. That year, Northwestern finished last in the Big Ten with a 2-16 record. Incredibly, Northwestern upset Michigan State 83–65. It was Northwestern's only victory during a 16-game span.

6. SANTA CLARA

Santa Clara, seeded fifteenth, was a 20-point underdog in a first-round game against second-seeded Arizona in the 1993 NCAA tournament. Arizona was upset 64–61, despite a stretch in which the Wildcats scored 25 consecutive points.

7. UNIVERSITY OF RICHMOND

Fifteenth-seeded Richmond was given little chance of defeating second-seeded Syracuse in the first round of the 1991

NCAA tournament. Nevertheless, Richmond upset Syracuse 73–69.

8. COPPIN STATE

Another 15-seed that upset a two seed was Coppin State. They defeated South Carolina 78–65 in the first round of the 1997 NCAA tournament.

9. MANHATTAN

In 1958, top-ranked West Virginia was upset by unranked Manhattan College 89–84 in the first round of the NCAA tournament. The Mountaineers' All-American guard, Jerry West, was held to 10 points.

10. VILLANOVA

The University of Pennsylvania carried a perfect 26-0 record entering their game against Villanova in the East Coast regional final of the 1971 NCAA tournament. Penn had three future NBA players in its lineup: Dave Wohl, Corky Calhoun, and Phil Hankinson. Howard Porter scored 35 points as Villanova upset Pennsylvania 90–47.

College's Greatest Games

These are the 10 most memorable games in college basketball history.

1. HOUSTON–UCLA

The January 20, 1968, matchup of UCLA and Houston was billed as The Game of the Century. The meeting of college basketball's top two teams also featured the top two players, UCLA's Lew Alcindor and Houston's Elvin Hayes. The Big E scored 39 points as Houston upset UCLA 71–69. Alcindor, hampered by an eye injury, was held to 15 points.

2. DUKE–KENTUCKY

In what is often called the greatest game in college basketball history, Duke and Kentucky met on March 28, 1992, in the East regional final of the NCAA tournament. With two seconds left in overtime, Kentucky's Sean Woods made a basket to give Kentucky a 103–102 lead. Duke's Grant Hill then threw a length-of-the-court pass to Christian Laettner. Laettner's turnaround jumper from the top of the key at the buzzer gave the Blue Devils a thrilling 104–103 victory. Duke went on to win the national championship.

3. NORTH CAROLINA-KANSAS

Undefeated North Carolina met Kansas in the championship of the 1957 NCAA tournament. The game showcased two of the nation's leading scorers, Wilt Chamberlain of Kansas and Lennie Rosenbluth of North Carolina. Rosenbluth scored 20 points as North Carolina edged Kansas 54–53 in triple overtime. Chamberlain tallied 23 points in the losing cause.

4. NOTRE DAME-UCLA

UCLA brought a record 88-game winning streak into a January 1974 matchup against Notre Dame. The Fighting Irish scored the game's last 12 points as they ended UCLA's winning streak, 71–70. Gary Brokaw's 25 points led the Irish in scoring.

5. NORTH CAROLINA STATE-UCLA

The UCLA Bruins, coached by John Wooden, were favored to win their eighth consecutive NCAA title in 1974. In the semifinal game, UCLA was matched against North Carolina State. David Thompson scored 28 points and Tom Burleson added 20 as the Wolfpack outlasted the Bruins 80–77 in double overtime.

6. NORTH CAROLINA STATE-MARYLAND

The March 9, 1974, game between North Carolina State and Maryland was one of the best-played in college basketball history. The Atlantic Coast Conference championship was on the line. Despite shooting better than 60 percent, Maryland lost to North Carolina State 103–100 in overtime.

7. MICHIGAN STATE–INDIANA STATE

Undefeated Indiana State met Michigan State in the championship game of the 1979 NCAA tournament. It marked the first meeting of Indiana State's Larry Bird and Michigan State's Magic Johnson. Johnson outscored Bird 24 to 19 as Michigan State won 75–64.

8. CINCINNATI–OHIO STATE

Ohio State, the defending national champion, faced Cincinnati in the 1961 NCAA title game. Ohio State entered the contest with a 27-game winning streak, while Cincinnati had won 20 in a row. Jerry Lucas scored 27 points for the Buckeyes, but four Bearcats scored in double figures as Cincinnati upset Ohio State 70–65 in overtime. The next season, the two Ohio teams met in a rematch that was also won by Cincinnati, 71–59.

9. NORTH CAROLINA STATE–HOUSTON

Most experts believed that the 1983 NCAA championship game between Houston and North Carolina State was a mismatch. Houston, nicknamed Phi Slamma Jamma for the team's dunking prowess, was led by Hakeem Olajuwon and Clyde Drexler. They were overwhelming favorites against a North Carolina State team that had lost 10 games during the season. With time running out, North Carolina State's Dereck Whittenburg threw up a desperation 30-footer. Teammate Lorenzo Charles caught the errant shot and laid it in to give the Wolfpack a 54–52 victory over the stunned Cougars.

10. **VILLANOVA-GEORGETOWN**

Georgetown, the defending national champion, was an overwhelming favorite to repeat in 1985. In the championship game, they faced Villanova, a team that had lost 10 times during the regular season. Eight-seeded Villanova shot 79 percent from the field, dethroning Georgetown 66–64.

Scoring Machines

When it came to scoring, these players were nearly unstoppable.

1. BEVO FRANCIS

Clarence "Bevo" Francis never played in the NBA, but he set collegiate scoring records that may never be broken. Playing for tiny Rio Grande College in Ohio, the 6'9" Francis averaged more than 50 points a game as a freshman and 46.5 points as a sophomore. He scored 116 points in a game against Ashland (Kentucky) Junior College. On February 2, 1954, Francis racked up 113 points in a 134–91 victory over Hillsdale College of Michigan. (If the three-point rule had been in effect, Francis might have scored 150 points.) In two other games, Francis tallied more than 80 points. Although the college's student enrollment was less than 100, Rio Grande defeated major schools such as Wake Forest and Providence. Francis left college after his sophomore season to play for the Boston Whirlwinds, a professional team that served as an opponent for the touring Harlem Globetrotters.

2. WILT CHAMBERLAIN

Wilt Chamberlain led the NBA in scoring during his first seven seasons. He averaged 50.4 points for the Philadelphia Warriors during the 1961–62 season. Chamberlain set an NBA single-game record when he scored 100 points against the New York Knicks that year. He scored 60 points or more 15 times and topped the 50 mark 45 times in the season. The next year, Chamberlain averaged 44.8 points per game.

3. FRANK SELVY

Furman's Frank Selvy averaged 41.7 points per game during the 1953–54 season. On February 13, 1954, Selvy set an NCAA record by scoring 100 points in a game against Newberry College.

4. PETE MARAVICH

Pete Maravich rewrote the college scoring record books during his career at Louisiana State from 1967 to 1970. His 44.2 career scoring average is an NCAA record. Maravich scored 50 points or more in 28 games. On February 21, 1970, he racked up 64 points in a 121–105 loss to Kentucky.

5. PAUL ARIZIN

Villanova's Paul Arizin was a first-team All-American in 1950. He scored 85 points in a game against the Philadelphia Air Materials Center. Five times Arizin scored 50 points or more in a game.

6. EARL MONROE

Earl "The Pearl" Monroe averaged 41.5 points per game during the 1966–67 season. He led Winston-Salem State to the NAIA championship.

7. JOHNNY NEUMANN

Johnny Neumann played only one season of college basketball, but what a season it was. Neumann averaged 40.1 points per game for the University of Mississippi during the 1970–71 campaign. He left college after one year to sign with the Memphis Pros of the ABA.

8. RICK MOUNT

Rick Mount of Purdue was one of the most deadly shooters in college basketball history. Mount averaged 35.4 points per game during the 1969–70 season. He set a Big Ten single-game record with a 61-point performance against Iowa.

9. BILL MCGILL

A two-time All-American at Utah, Bill "The Hill" McGill topped the nation in scoring in 1962 with a 38.8 average. The previous season, McGill had led Utah to a Final Four appearance.

10. GEORGE MIKAN

George Mikan was professional basketball's first great scorer. The big man led the league in scoring during his first six seasons.

One-Man Teams

In a 1945 NIT game, DePaul's George Mikan scored 53 points in a game against Rhode Island. His output equaled the total of the entire Rhode Island team. Here are some more one-man teams.

1. MATS WERMELIN

Thirteen-year-old Mats Wermelin was a one-boy team in a boys tournament played in Stockholm, Sweden. On February 5, 1974, he scored every point in a 272–0 victory.

2. JOHN BARBER

In 1953, John Barber of Los Angeles State totaled 188 points in a 206–82 victory over the Champion College junior varsity. Barber scored 106 points more than the opposing team.

3. MARIE BOYD

On February 24, 1929, Marie Boyd set a girls' high-school record with 156 points in a game. Boyd scored all but seven of her team's points in Lonaconing (Maryland) Central High's 163–3 rout of Ursuline Academy. Boyd sank 77 field goals in the game.

4. FRANK SELVY

Frank Selvy scored 100 points as Furman defeated Newberry College 149–95 in a game played on February 13, 1954. Selvy outscored the Newberry team in his record-breaking performance, making 41 of 66 field-goal attempts and adding 18 free throws.

5. WILT CHAMBERLAIN

Wilt Chamberlain scored 100 points in a game against the New York Knicks on March 2, 1962. The Philadelphia Warriors' center was so unstoppable that four different Knicks guarded him during the game. But Darrall Imhoff, Dave Budd, Johnny Green, and Cleveland Buckner had no luck stopping Chamberlain.

6. CHRISTIAN STEINMETZ

Wisconsin's Christian Steinmetz scored 44 points in an 80–10 win against Beloit College. During the 1904–05 season, Steinmetz outscored the opposition by 23 points.

7. OSCAR ROBERTSON

On January 9, 1958, Cincinnati's Oscar Robertson outscored the entire Seton Hall team during a game played at Madison Square Garden. Robertson totaled 56 points in the 118–54 victory.

8. HANK LUISETTI

Hank Luisetti of Stanford is the player who popularized the one-handed shot. His prodigious scoring displays doomed the two-handed set shot. On January 1, 1938, Luisetti notched 50 points as Stanford crushed Duquesne 92–27.

9. **JOHN ANDERSON**

John Anderson was a turn-of-the-century scoring star at Bucknell. During the 1903 season, he scored 80 points in a 159–5 trouncing of the Philadelphia College of Pharmacy.

10. **WILLIAM MILLER**

Michigan's William Miller scored 14 points in a 1921 game against Indiana. What's so great about that? They were the only points in Michigan's 14–0 win.

Record Breakers

Not every college basketball record was set by Pete Maravich.

1. KEVIN BRADSHAW

Kevin Bradshaw of U.S. International scored 72 points in a January 5, 1991, game against Loyola Marymount. The 72 points set a single-game record against a Division I opponent. Bradshaw's heroics were not enough, however, as Loyola Marymount defeated U.S. International 186–140.

2. BILL CHAMBERS

William and Mary's Bill Chambers holds the record for the most rebounds in a college game. He pulled down 51 boards against Virginia on February 14, 1953.

3. AVERY JOHNSON

In 1988, Avery Johnson of Southern University of Louisiana set a college record by averaging 13.3 assists per game. He shares the single-game record with 22 assists against Texas Southern on January 25, 1988.

4. **MOOKIE BLAYLOCK**

Daron "Mookie" Blaylock set the college record with 13 steals in a game against Centenary on December 12, 1987. A year later, the Oklahoma guard tied his record with a 13-steal performance against Loyola Marymount. In 1988, Blaylock set a single-season record for steals with 150.

5. **STEVE MYERS**

Steve Myers of Pacific Lutheran made the longest shot in college basketball history on January 16, 1970. Standing out of bounds, Myers sank a length-of-the-court shot. The 92-footer, although technically illegal, was allowed to count.

6. **STEVE JOHNSON**

The record for the highest field-goal percentage in a season belongs to Steve Johnson of Oregon State. During 1981, Johnson made 235 of 315 shots for a .746 mark.

7. **CRAIG COLLINS**

Penn State's Craig Collins set the record for highest free-throw percentage in a season. He missed only four free throws during the 1985 campaign, posting a .959 percentage.

8. **RAY VOELKEL**

Ray Voelkel of American University made 25 consecutive field goals during a nine-game span in 1978. The streak began on November 16 and ended on November 24.

9. **TODD LESLIE**

Northwestern's Todd Leslie made 15 consecutive three-point shots in December 1990. The record streak lasted from December 15 until December 28.

10. **STEPHEN SCHEFFLER**

Purdue's Stephen Scheffler set the record for the highest career field-goal percentage. From 1987 to 1990, he made 408 of 596 shots for a .685 mark.

Mules, Stags, and Vagabond Kings

The Boston Celtics, Los Angeles Lakers, and New York Knicks are three of the NBA's best-known franchises. The following are some of basketball's lesser-known teams.

1. TRI-CITIES BLACKHAWKS

The Tri-Cities Blackhawks joined the NBA in 1949. The team represented two cities in Illinois (Moline and Rock Island) and one in Iowa (Davenport). In 1951, the team moved to Milwaukee. Since then, the Hawks have played in St. Louis and are currently in Atlanta.

2. SHEBOYGAN REDSKINS

The Sheboygan Redskins were part of the National Basketball League from 1938 to 1949. In 1949, the Wisconsin team joined the NBA. After finishing the season with a 22–40 record, the Redskins folded.

3. ANDERSON PACKERS

The Packers are one of the NFL's most famed franchises and one of the NBA's most obscure. The Anderson Packers were an NBL team from 1946 to 1949. The Indiana team played in the NBA during the 1949–50 season.

4. WATERLOO HAWKS

Another team that played only one season in the NBA was the Waterloo (Iowa) Hawks. The Hawks had a 19-43 record during the 1949–50 campaign.

5. PROVIDENCE STEAMROLLERS

The Providence Steamrollers were charter members of the NBA in 1946. The Rhode Island team remained in the league until 1949.

6. NATIONAL BASKETBALL LEAGUE

The National Basketball League, forerunner of the NBA, was formed in 1937. Some of the teams that played in the NBL over the years were the Akron Firestone Non-Skids, Akron Goodyear Wing Foots, Chicago American Gears, Cleveland Allmen Transfers, Columbia Athletic Supply, Detroit Vagabond Kings, Indianapolis Kautskys, Kanakee Gallagher Trojans, Richard King Clothiers, and The Toledo Jim White Chevrolets.

7. AMERICAN BASKETBALL LEAGUE

The American Basketball League was a professional league in the mid-1930s. Teams that played in the ABL include the Brooklyn Visitations, Philadelphia Hebrews, and the Newark Mules.

8. **PITTSBURGH IRONMEN**

A charter member of the NBA, the Pittsburgh Ironmen dropped out of the league after a 15-45 record during the 1946–47 season.

9. **ST. LOUIS BOMBERS**

Another charter member of the NBA, the St. Louis Bombers, remained in the league until 1950.

10. **CHICAGO STAGS**

Long before the Bulls, the city of Chicago had a franchise in the NBA. The Chicago Stags played in the league from 1946 until 1950.

They Never Won an NBA Title

The careers of stars are often measured by how many championship teams they played on. Wilt Chamberlain was a more dominating center than Bill Russell, but he played on two NBA champions compared to Russell's 11. None of these superstars played on even one NBA champion.

1. ELGIN BAYLOR

Elgin Baylor helped revolutionize the NBA with his athletic play. Baylor averaged 27.4 points per game during his career with the Lakers from 1958 to 1972, but he had the misfortune of playing during the heyday of the Boston Celtics. Eight times the Lakers reached the NBA finals, and eight times they lost. The year after Baylor retired, the Lakers won the NBA title.

2. CHARLES BARKLEY

Charles Barkley was one of the best forwards in the NBA during his career, which lasted from 1984 to 2000. Barkley played for Philadelphia, Phoenix, and Houston. In 1993, Barkley led Phoenix to the NBA finals, but the Suns lost. Teamed with Hakeem Olajuwon on the Houston Rockets during his final four seasons, Barkley failed to win the elusive title.

Dick Raphael

Elgin Baylor, *right,* helped revolutionize the game with his athletic play, but he never had the good fortune to win a NBA title.

3. KARL MALONE

The quintessential power forward, Karl Malone has starred with the Utah Jazz since 1985. In 2000, he became the NBA's second leading all-time scorer. The Mailman reached the NBA finals only once. In 1997, Malone and the Jazz fell victim to the magic of Michael Jordan and the Chicago Bulls.

4. JOHN STOCKTON

A member of the Utah Jazz since 1984, John Stockton is one of the best point guards to ever play the game. The NBA's all-time leader in assists and steals, Stockton, like teammate Malone, is still awaiting his first championship.

5. GEORGE GERVIN

George Gervin played for San Antonio and Chicago during his NBA career, from 1976 to 1986. The Iceman won two scoring titles but no NBA championships.

6. PATRICK EWING

Patrick Ewing has been one of the NBA's premier centers since he entered the league in 1985. He played 15 seasons in New York. The Knicks nearly won the title in 1994 before losing to the Houston Rockets in seven games.

7. PETE MARAVICH

College basketball's greatest scorer during his years at Louisiana State, Pete Maravich was the NBA scoring champion in 1977. He played 10 seasons in the league with Atlanta and New Orleans, but he never played in the NBA finals.

8. **BOB LANIER**

An eight-time All-Star, center Bob Lanier played for the Detroit Pistons and Milwaukee Bucks from 1973 to 1984. Lanier led his teams to five divisional titles, but he never played on an NBA champion.

9. **ALEX ENGLISH**

One of the most prolific scorers in NBA history, Alex English was the league scoring champion in 1983. From 1976 to 1991, English played for Milwaukee, Indiana, Denver, and Dallas, but he never played on a championship team.

10. **ARTIS GILMORE**

At 7'2", Artis Gilmore was one of the NBA's most intimidating centers. Gilmore played for Chicago and San Antonio during his dozen seasons in the NBA. He retired in 1988 without ever playing on a championship team.

International Basketball Association

The NBA has gone international in recent years. In the 2000 NBA draft, several foreign-born players were selected, including Mamadov N'Diaye (Senegal), Eduardo Najera (Mexico), Hanno Mottola (Finland), Soumaila Samake (Mali), and Hidayet Turkoglu (Turkey). Other NBA players who were born abroad include Arvydas Sabonis (Lithuania), Tariq Abdul-Wahad (France), Lazaro Borrell (Cuba), Adonal Foyle (Grenadines), Rasha Nesterovic (Slovenia), Olden Polynice (Haiti), Vitaly Potapenko (Ukraine), Vladimir Stepania (Republic of Georgia), and Bill Wennington (Canada).

1. HAKEEM OLAJUWON

Hakeem Olajuwon was born in Lagos, Nigeria. Olajuwon did not take up basketball until near the end of his high-school years. A natural talent, Olajuwon led the University of Houston to two NCAA finals and the Houston Rockets to two NBA championships.

2. PATRICK EWING

Born in Kingston, Jamaica, Patrick Ewing played on a national championship team at Georgetown in 1984. Ewing's career with the New York Knicks earned him a selection as one of the NBA's 50 greatest players.

3. DETLEF SCHREMPF

One of the first outstanding foreign-born players in the NBA, German Detlef Schrempf played his college basketball at the University of Washington. Since his entry into the NBA in 1985, Schrempf has starred for Dallas, Indiana, and Seattle.

4. TONI KUKOC

Toni Kukoc had the reputation of being the best player in Europe. The Croatian starred in the Italian League before joining the Bulls in 1993. An outstanding shooter, Kukoc was a major reason that the Bulls won three consecutive NBA titles from 1996 to 1998.

5. LUC LONGLEY

A native of Australia, Luc Longley was a teammate of Kukoc's on three Chicago Bulls championship teams. The 7'2" center was twice a member of the Australian Olympic team.

6. VLADE DIVAC

Seven-foot Vlade Divac was a member of the silver-medal Yugoslavian Olympic teams in 1988 and 1996. Divac starred for the Los Angeles Lakers from 1989 to 1996 and also played for Charlotte and Sacramento.

7. MANUTE BOL

Manute Bol was born in Sudan. The Dinka tribesman was brought to America to develop his basketball skills. Known as "The Dinka Destroyer," the 7'6" center became one of the NBA's best shot blockers.

8. GHEORGHE MURESAN

At 7'7", Romanian Gheorghe Muresan is one of the tallest players in NBA history. Muresan played in the French League before being drafted by the Washington Bullets in 1993.

9. RIK SMITS

Rik Smits is yet another seven-foot center from Europe. The Dutchman, known for his fine shooting touch, starred for the Indiana Pacers from 1988 to 2000.

10. DIKEMBE MUTOMBO

Like Patrick Ewing, Dikembe Mutombo is an outstanding foreign-born center who played his college ball at Georgetown. Born in Zaire, Mutombo has been one of the NBA's best defensive players and rebounders for a decade.

Role Players

Not everyone can be a star. Many players have long and successful NBA careers without ever reaching stardom. Every player on this list has played in the NBA at least 10 seasons without ever averaging in double figures.

1. BILL WENNINGTON

Bill Wennington never averaged more than seven points in a season, but for 15 years he was a valuable bench player for Chicago, Dallas, and Sacramento. The seven-foot center played on championship teams with the Chicago Bulls in 1996, 1997, and 1998.

2. STEVE KERR

Although he never averaged double figures in a season, Steve Kerr could put points on the scoreboard in a hurry. Kerr led the NBA in three-point field-goal percentage in 1990 and 1995 and also holds the career mark. His timely shooting helped the Chicago Bulls win three straight championships from 1996 to 1998. Traded to the San Antonio Spurs in 1998, he played on his fourth consecutive NBA champion.

3. CHRIS DUDLEY

Chris Dudley was drafted by the Cleveland Cavaliers in 1987 in the fourth round. The 6'11" Dudley, who played his college ball at Yale, has been a backup center for Cleveland, New Jersey, Portland, and New York. An excellent rebounder, Dudley has played more than a dozen years in the NBA despite being one of the poorest free-throw shooters in league history.

4. CALDWELL JONES

Caldwell Jones played for Philadelphia, Houston, Chicago, Portland, and San Antonio between 1976 and 1990. He averaged only 6.2 points per game during his career, but he was one of the league's best shot blockers. Jones was named to the NBA All-Defensive Team in 1981 and 1982.

5. JOE KLEINE

Seven-foot center Joe Kleine played for Sacramento, Boston, Phoenix, Los Angeles, New Jersey, Chicago, and Portland from 1985 to 2000. The highlight of Kleine's professional career was being a reserve on the 1998 NBA champion Chicago Bulls.

6. DAVID WINGATE

David Wingate was a member of the national championship team at Georgetown in 1984. Since 1986, Wingate has played for Philadelphia, San Antonio, Washington, Charlotte, Seattle, and New York. The 6'5" Wingate was especially valuable off the bench because he could play both guard and forward.

7. **WILL PERDUE**

Will Perdue is another seven-foot backup center who has enjoyed a long career in the NBA. Perdue played on NBA championship teams with Chicago in 1991, 1992, and 1993. In 1999, Perdue was David Robinson's backup on the championship San Antonio Spurs.

8. **CHUCKY BROWN**

From 1989 to 2000, Chucky Brown played for Cleveland, Los Angeles, New Jersey, Dallas, Houston, Phoenix, Milwaukee, Atlanta, Charlotte, and San Antonio. The well-traveled forward was a member of the champion 1995 Houston Rockets.

9. **JUD BUECHLER**

One of the reasons for the championship reign in Chicago during the 1990s was a solid bench. Guard/forward Jud Buechler provided valuable minutes for the championship teams of 1996, 1997, and 1998. Buechler, who began his career with New Jersey in 1990, has also played for San Antonio, Golden State, and Detroit.

10. **DUANE CAUSWELL**

During the 1990s, Duane Causwell played center for the Sacramento Kings and the Miami Heat. The seven-foot center averaged five points and four rebounds per game during his career.

Like Father, Like Son

All of these professional players produced sons who played in the NBA.

1. RICK BARRY

Rick Barry was one of the greatest scorers in basketball history. He led the NCAA, ABA, and NBA in scoring and played on a championship team at Golden State in 1975. Three of Barry's sons have also seen action in the NBA. Brent Barry has played guard for the Los Angeles Clippers, Miami Heat, Chicago Bulls, and Seattle Super Sonics. Guard Drew Barry has played for the Atlanta Hawks, Seattle Super Sonics, and Golden State Warriors. Jon Barry has been a guard for the Milwaukee Bucks, Golden State Warriors, Atlanta Hawks, Los Angeles Lakers, and Sacramento Kings.

2. PRESS MARAVICH

Press Maravich played guard for Pittsburgh in the NBA's inaugural year. He averaged 4.6 points per game during the 1946–47 season. His son, Pete, was college basketball's most prolific scorer and averaged 24.2 points a game during his 10-year NBA career with Atlanta, New Orleans, and Boston.

3. DOLPH SCHAYES

Dolph Schayes was one of the best and most durable players of the 1950s. He played for Syracuse and Philadelphia from 1948 to 1964. The Hall of Famer set an NBA record by appearing in 706 consecutive games. His son, Danny, although not as good a player as his father, also had a long NBA career. He entered the league with Utah in 1981 and played for nearly two decades. Danny Schayes averaged 13.9 points for Denver in 1988.

4. JELLY BEAN BRYANT

Joe "Jelly Bean" Bryant played in the NBA from 1975 to 1983 with Philadelphia, San Diego, and Houston. His best season was 1982, when he averaged 11.8 points for San Diego. Son Kobe is one of the NBA's top scorers. The young superstar was a major reason why the Los Angeles Lakers won the NBA championships in 2000 and 2001.

5. JIMMY WALKER

Jimmy Walker played guard for Detroit, Houston, and Kansas City/Omaha from 1967 to 1976. In both 1970 and 1972, he averaged more than 20 points a game for the Detroit Pistons. Son Jalen Rose is a rising star in the NBA. He was named the Most Improved Player in 2000 when he averaged 18.2 points per game for the Indiana Pacers.

6. JIM PAXSON SR.

Jim Paxson Sr. played for the Minneapolis Lakers and Cincinnati Royals from 1956 to 1958. He averaged nearly 10 points a game for Cincinnati in 1958. Two of his sons, Jim and John, had long careers in the NBA. Jim Paxson Jr. was an outstanding player for Portland in the 1980s. He averaged more than 21 points per game in both 1983 and 1984. John Paxson came into the league in 1983 with San Antonio, but he is best remembered for his clutch shooting as a member of the Chicago Bulls.

7. ERNIE VANDEWEGHE

Ernie Vandeweghe played for the New York Knicks from 1949 to 1956, averaging 12 points per game in 1953. His son, Kiki Vandeweghe, was one of the NBA's top scorers of the 1980s. His best season was 1984 when he averaged 29.4 points per game for the Denver Nuggets.

8. BOB FERRY

Bob Ferry played in the NBA from 1959 to 1969 with St. Louis, Detroit, and Baltimore. Ferry averaged nearly 14 points per game for Detroit in 1962. Danny Ferry, his son, played forward for the Cleveland Cavaliers from 1990 to 2000, averaging 13.3 points in 1996.

9. WAYNE CHAPMAN

Wayne Chapman played for Kentucky, Denver, and Indiana in the ABA from 1968 to 1972. Son Rex has played in the NBA for Charlotte, Washington, Miami, and Phoenix. He averaged in double figures each year from 1988 to 1999.

10. GEORGE MIKAN

George Mikan was the NBA's first great center. He led the Minneapolis Lakers to five NBA championships and led the league in scoring six consecutive years. Mikan's son, Larry, played for the Cleveland Cavaliers during the 1970–71 season.

Calling the Shots

Every player has his own way of shooting the ball. The players on this list perfected shots that became their signature moves.

1. HANK LUISETTI

Stanford's Hank Luisetti developed his running one-handed shot while playing at Galileo High School in San Francisco. A prolific scorer during his career at Stanford from 1935 to 1938, Luisetti was the first to perfect the one-handed shot. It revolutionized basketball, making for a higher-scoring, faster-paced game.

2. KAREEM ABDUL-JABBAR

Kareem Abdul-Jabbar (Lew Alcindor) was such a prolific scorer that the dunk shot was banned in college during his years at UCLA. He proved to be just as unstoppable in the NBA. He developed a skyhook that was almost impossible to defend. Abdul-Jabbar scored 38,387 points in his pro career, easily the most in NBA history.

3. **BOB HOUBREGS**

The skyhook was Abdul-Jabbar's version of the hook shot, popular for decades with the game's big men. One of the greatest hook-shot artists was Bob Houbregs. An All-American at the University of Washington, Houbregs averaged 25.8 points per game during the 1952–53 season. His graceful hook shot helped ensure his election to the Basketball Hall of Fame.

4. **WILT CHAMBERLAIN**

Wilt Chamberlain set scoring records that will probably never be broken. He is the only player ever to score 100 points in an NBA game and average 50 points per game for a season. One of Chamberlain's most devastating offensive weapons was a finger-roll shot that helped earn him the nickname The Big Dipper.

5. **JOE FULKS**

Joe Fulks had an offensive arsenal that was unrivaled in his day. During the late 1940s, Jumpin' Joe was pro basketball's most feared scorer. He used the turnaround jumper and the two-handed scoop shot to score points in record numbers. Fulks' jumper was known as "Ear Shot" because he reached back and launched it from behind his ear.

6. **SAM JONES**

Sam Jones played on 10 Boston Celtics championship teams. Jones was probably the greatest bank-shot artist in basketball history. Through countless hours of practice, he learned how to bank shots off the backboard from almost every possible angle.

7. **DOLPH SCHAYES**

The two-handed set shot was the shot of choice during the early decades of basketball. One of the last great two-handed set-shot masters was Dolph Schayes. He perfected the shot after he broke his left wrist and needed to use both hands to shoot. Schayes used the set shot to average 18.2 points per game during his NBA career. He was elected to the Basketball Hall of Fame in 1973.

8. **OSCAR ROBERTSON**

Oscar Robertson led the nation in scoring all three seasons he played with the University of Cincinnati. Averaging more than 25 points per game during his professional career, "The Big O" was one of the best shooting guards in NBA history. Robertson's one-handed push shot was his trademark.

9. **RICK BARRY**

Rick Barry was arguably the greatest free-throw shooter in NBA history. He converted more than 90 percent of his free throws for six consecutive seasons. He attributed his success to his underhanded delivery. Barry lowered the ball between his legs and scooped it toward the basket.

10. **KEN SAILORS**

The jump shot is the standard in basketball, but it has not always been that way. Early shooters stood flat-footed as they heaved the ball toward the basket. The man who helped popularize the jump shot was Ken Sailors. He played for the University of Wyoming in the early 1940s. The jump shot was more accurate than the set shot and more difficult to defend.

Doctors of Dunk

The dunk is basketball's most explosive shot. These players were the masters of dunk.

1. DARRYL DAWKINS

Darryl Dawkins may not have been the greatest dunker of all time, but he was certainly the most enthusiastic. In 1979, he shattered two glass backboards with his thunderous slam dunks. Dawkins gave names to his dunks, such as "Look Out Below," "In Your Face Disgrace," and "The Left-Handed Spine-Chiller Supreme." As his dunks became more spectacular, so did their names. Dawkins christened his backboard-breaking dunk the "No Playin', Get Out of the Wayin', Backboard Swayin', Game Delayin' Dunk." When Kansas City's Bill Robinzine complained after being slightly cut by a piece of broken glass from the shattered backboard, Dawkins renamed the dunk, "The Chocolate Thunder Flyin', Robinzine Cryin', Teeth Shakin', Glass Breakin', Rump Roastin', Bun Toastin', Wham Bam, I Am Jam."

2. CHUCK CONNORS

More than 30 years before Darryl Dawkins made headlines with his backboard-shattering dunks, Chuck Connors of the Boston Celtics brought down the backboard with a dunk. Connors shattered the backboard while warming up for a November 5, 1946, game against the Chicago Stags at the Boston Arena. Connors's professional basketball career was less spectacular, but he later gained fame as a television and movie star.

3. HELICOPTER HENTZ

Charles "Helicopter" Hentz was one of the most colorful players in the history of the ABA, a league known for its showmanship. Hentz was given the nickname "Helicopter" because of his incredible hang time. On November 6, 1970, the Pittsburgh Condors' forward shattered two glass backboards in a game against the Carolina Cougars in Raleigh, North Carolina. Carolina won 122–107. The Cougars sent Hertz a bill for $750, but he refused to pay.

4. JULIUS ERVING

Julius Erving turned the dunk into an art form. By the time Erving was in the seventh grade, he could dunk the ball, and by the time he graduated Roosevelt High School in New York, he had an entire arsenal of dunks. Dr. J dazzled fans in the ABA and NBA with his spectacular slams.

5. JACKIE JACKSON

Some of the best basketball is played on the playgrounds of New York City. Jackie Jackson became a legend in the Bedford Stuyvesant area with his fantastic leaping ability. He

Julius Erving, a.k.a. Dr. J, turned the dunk into an art form long before anyone had ever heard of Michael Jordan. Here he flies by Larry Bird for the finish.

performed a dunk entirely his own. Jackson went airborne at the foul line, lowered the ball to his waist, raised it over his head, and then slammed it home. Jackson named his dunk "The Double Doober, with a Cherry on Top."

6. DARRELL GRIFFITH

The 1980 Louisville Cardinals were known as The Doctors of Dunk. The high-flying Cardinals defeated UCLA 59–54 to win the NCAA championship. The team's leading scorer and dominant dunker was Darrell Griffith, whose monster dunks earned him the nickname "Dr. Dunkenstein."

7. SPUD WEBB

The annual slam-dunk competition at the NBA All-Star Game featured the league's greatest dunkers. The surprise winner in 1986 was Atlanta Hawks guard Anthony "Spud" Webb. The 5'7" Spud proved that you do not have to be a big man to be a great dunker.

8. GEORGEANN WELLS

The first woman to dunk a ball in a game was West Virginia's Georgeann Wells. She performed the feat on December 21, 1984, in a 110–82 victory over the University of Charleston.

9. MICHAEL JORDAN

No list of great dunkers would be complete without Michael Jordan. "Air" Jordan literally brought the game of basketball to new heights with his gravity-defying leaps. Defenders appeared helpless each time Jordan floated to the basket for another sensational slam dunk.

10. JOHN WARREN

The 1970 Cleveland Cavaliers was one of the worst teams in NBA history. Nicknamed "The Cadavers" because they were usually dead meat, the expansion team finished the year with a dreadful 15-67 record. The Cavaliers' futility was personified in a game against Portland. Cleveland's John Warren tried to relieve his frustration with a rousing slam dunk. The only problem was that he had dunked the ball into the wrong basket.

The Best There Was

These players were without peer in what they did best.

1. WILT CHAMBERLAIN

Wilt Chamberlain can lay claim to being the best in two of basketball's most important categories. The seven-time NBA scoring champion is the only player to score more than 4,000 points in a season. Eleven times Chamberlain led the league in rebounding. For his career, he averaged nearly 23 rebounds per game.

2. JOHN STOCKTON

Utah guard John Stockton also is tops in two major NBA categories. Stockton is the all-time leader in career assists and steals.

3. BILL SHARMAN

The NBA has had its share of great free-throw shooters. You could make a case for Rick Barry, Larry Bird, or Calvin Murphy as the all-time best. Boston guard Bill Sharman was certainly one of the best. He led the league in free-throw percentage seven times and made 93.2 percent of his foul shots during the 1958–59 season. His .911 free-throw percentage in the playoffs demonstrated his ability to perform under pressure.

4. BILL RUSSELL

Sharman's teammate in Boston, Bill Russell, proved that defense wins championships. Russell was the man-in-the-middle for the Celtics on 11 championship teams. If he did not block your shot, he would almost certainly get the rebound. In 165 playoff games, Russell averaged nearly 25 rebounds per game.

5. MARQUES HAYNES

Who was the greatest dribbler in basketball history? The name that immediately comes to mind is Marques Haynes. He entertained audiences around the world as a member of the Harlem Globetrotters with his remarkable ball handling and fantastic dribbling skills. The fastest dribbler in basketball, Haynes could dribble the ball three times per second.

6. DALE ELLIS

The three-point shot has become one of basketball's most important offensive weapons. The NBA's all-time leader in three-point baskets is Dale Ellis. Ellis displayed his long-range shooting skills by winning the 1989 AT&T Long Distance Shootout at the NBA All-Star Game.

7. JOHN HAVLICEK

The Celtics had a great tradition of sixth men. From Frank Ramsey to Kevin McHale, Boston usually had the best first man off the bench. Perhaps the greatest sixth man in NBA history was Boston's John Havlicek. The Celtics' all-time leading scorer, Havlicek was also one of the game's greatest defenders. His inspired play helped the Celtics to eight NBA championships.

8. **MARK EATON**

Not surprisingly, seven-foot centers are the game's dominant shot blockers. Two of the best of all time were Kareem Abdul-Jabbar and Manute Bol. Utah's 7' 4" center, Mark Eaton, was also one of the league's most intimidating shot blockers. Between 1984 and 1988, Eaton led the league in blocks four times.

9. **A. C. GREEN**

A. C. Green is the iron man of professional basketball. Entering the 2000 season, Green had played in a record 1,110 games. The streak began on November 19, 1986.

10. **ARTIS GILMORE**

Artis Gilmore may not have been the best shooter in NBA history, but he was the most efficient. Gilmore made 5,732 of 9,570 field-goal attempts for a record .599 percentage.

Showtime

Each of these players alone were worth the price of admission.

1. DOMINIQUE WILKINS

Dominique Wilkins earned the nickname "The Human Highlight Film" because of his flair for spectacular play. Wilkins always seemed to jump higher and fly farther than anyone else. He led the NBA in scoring with the Atlanta Hawks in 1986. Twice he averaged more than 30 points per game and averaged more than 25 points 10 consecutive years.

2. HOT ROD HUNDLEY

Hot Rod Hundley may have been the biggest showboat in basketball history. At the University of West Virginia, Hundley averaged 26.6 points in his junior year, but it was his unique ball handling, passing, and shooting skills that made him a fan favorite. In a game against George Washington, he shot one free throw from behind his back and hook-shot another. Hot Rod executed his "praying mantis" shot from his knees. When he missed several shots in a row, Hundley climbed up on the basket support and looked through the net to see what went wrong. He rolled the ball up and down his arms and spun it on his finger to entertain the crowds. Hundley played in the NBA with the Lakers from 1957 to 1963.

3. BOB DAVIES

Bob Davies was known as the "Harrisburg Houdini." A spectacular passer who set the NBA record for assists with 20 in a game against Boston in 1955, Davies was the original showtime player. Decades before Pete Maravich, Davies wowed fans with his behind-the-back dribbling. A two-time All-American at Seton Hall, Davies was an eight-time All-Star with the Rochester Royals.

4. MEADOWLARK LEMON

Known as "The Clown Prince of Basketball," Meadowlark Lemon lived up to his name as a member of the Harlem Globetrotters. Lemon's comic routines entertained audiences for 20 years. His famous bits included switching a medicine ball for a basketball and throwing a bucket of confetti into the audience.

5. JASON WILLIAMS

One of the flashiest players in the NBA today is guard Jason Williams of the Sacramento Kings. Williams frequently is featured on evening highlight films with his behind-the-back passes and eye-catching moves to the basket.

6. WORLD B. FREE

Lloyd Free was nicknamed "All World" because of his phenomenal ability. He was so taken with the moniker that he legally changed his name to World B. Free. From 1979 to 1986, Free averaged more than 20 points per season in the NBA.

7. **EARL MONROE**

Earl Monroe's play demanded superlatives. Monroe was nicknamed "Black Magic" for his ability to create something from nothing. Earl "The Pearl" averaged more than 40 points per game in his final year of college at Winston-Salem and capped off his career as part of the Rolls Royce Backcourt (along with Walt Frazier) of the New York Knicks.

8. **MAGIC JOHNSON**

If Earl Monroe held fans spellbound with his "Black Magic," Earvin Johnson was simply known as Magic. At 6'9", Johnson combined the playmaking skills of a point guard with the power moves of a forward. Magic helped bring the era of "Showtime" to the Los Angeles Lakers in the 1980s.

9. **CONNIE HAWKINS**

Connie Hawkins became a legend on the playgrounds of New York City. Hawkins's style combined the free-wheeling brand of street basketball with the high-flying above-the-rim game that made him one of the NBA's biggest stars.

10. **CLYDE DREXLER**

Clyde Drexler first displayed his remarkable dunking technique as a member of the University of Houston's Phi Slamma Jamma teams. Clyde "The Glide" was one of the best one-on-one players in basketball history. An outstanding scorer, he averaged more than 20 points a game in his NBA career, which lasted from 1983 to 1998.

Totally Outrageous

Dennis Rodman is not the only outrageous figure in basketball.

1. DENNIS RODMAN

Sportscaster Roy Firestone said, "Every day is Halloween for Dennis Rodman." One of the NBA's greatest rebounders, Rodman was the undeniable king of self-promotion. On the court, Rodman kicked a cameraman in the groin, head-butted an official, and dyed his hair various colors. Off-court, he once dressed like a bride at a book signing for his auto-biography, *Bad As I Wanna Be,* and he had highly publicized romances with Madonna and Carmen Electra.

2. BOBBY KNIGHT

Bobby Knight coached Indiana to 661 victories, 11 Big Ten titles, and three national championships. Despite his success, Knight was always a controversial figure. He frequently had run-ins with the press. Knight once said, "Absolute silence is one thing a sportswriter can quote accurately." Always the diplomat, Knight also remarked, "Bury me upside down so critics can kiss my ass." On another occasion, he cracked a whip at a press conference, noting that "no motivational device is so effective." At the 1979 Pan American Games, Knight allegedly struck a Puerto Rican security guard and was convicted in absentia. In his most notorious outburst, he flung a plastic chair across the court in disgust during a game against Purdue. Knight's later years as Indiana coach were plagued by charges that he had physically and verbally abused some members of his team. According to reports, he had choked, head-butted, and kicked players. The Knight era at Indiana ended in September 2000 after he was involved in a confrontation with a student.

3. GLENN MARX

Glenn Marx, coach of Notre Dame of Louisiana, lost his temper, then lost a game against Daniel Murphy on November 4, 1979. His team was leading 67–61 with time running out when he was assessed three technical fouls. The irate coach refused to leave the court and was then assessed nine more technicals. Herb Simon made 11 of 12 free throws to give Daniel Murphy a shocking 72–67 victory.

4. WILT CHAMBERLAIN

Wilt Chamberlain was one of the greatest scorers in NBA history, and he didn't do too badly in his personal life, either. According to Chamberlain, he had more than 20,000 lovers. That's a different lover every night for 55 years. Apparently, Chamberlain double-teamed both on and off the court.

5. BENNY BORGMANN

Benny Borgmann was one of the best players of the 1920s. He led the American Basketball League in scoring from 1929 to 1931. Early in his career, Borgmann played in numerous local leagues, many of which had religious affiliations. When Borgmann played in a Jewish league, he was Jewish; in a Catholic league, he pretended to be Catholic. In reality, Borgmann was a Protestant.

6. DARRYL DAWKINS

Darryl Dawkins is best remembered for his backboard-shattering dunks, but he was also one of the most prolific foulers in NBA history. During the 1982–83 season, he set a record with 379 fouls. The next year, Dawkins broke his own record with 386 fouls.

7. MARVIN BARNES

Marvin Barnes was known as much for his eccentric behavior as he was for his basketball prowess. Barnes starred at Providence College before spending two productive years with St. Louis of the ABA. Barnes had an outrageous appetite for food and the good life. Even during his four seasons as a journeyman in the NBA, he displayed his love of expensive automobiles, colorful clothes, and attractive women.

8. WALT FRAZIER

Walt Frazier was one of the few basketball players who could match Marvin Barnes for his love of flashy clothes and exotic automobiles. Frazier was nicknamed "Clyde" after Clyde Barrow of the *Bonnie and Clyde* film because of his retro outfits. He liked to wear wide-brimmed hats, crushed velvet suits, and ride around in a Rolls Royce. An offensive threat and defensive standout, Frazier played guard on the New York Knicks championship teams of 1970 and 1973.

9. **MARK CUBAN**

Mark Cuban became a billionaire with his Internet company, Broadcast.com. Since buying the Dallas Mavericks, he has quickly become something of a maverick owner. Cuban has been extremely critical of NBA officials. To date, he's been fined more than $500,000 for his criticism of the officiating, which he describes as inconsistent.

10. **STEVE ALFORD**

All-American Steve Alford was penalized for his good looks. In 1985, he was suspended for a game for appearing in an unauthorized beefcake calendar. With their star player on the bench, the Hoosiers lost to Kentucky 63–58.

The Worm Turns

Without a doubt, Dennis "The Worm" Rodman is the most famous NBA player with a career scoring average of just over seven points. Here are 10 reasons why Dennis Rodman became a household name.

1. BAD AS I WANNA BE

In May 1995, Dennis Rodman hinted to reporters that his future bride might appear with him at a New York bookstore for the signing of his autobiography, *Bad As I Wanna Be.* As it turned out, Rodman arrived at the bookstore dressed as a bride himself. Rodman admitted, "I love dressing either way."

2. THE MIRAGE

When he was not playing basketball, Dennis Rodman loved the nightlife of Las Vegas. It was reported that he lost hundreds of thousands of dollars at the gaming tables. Rodman was sued by the dealer of a table when he allegedly rubbed the man's genitals for luck before tossing the dice.

3. EUGENE AMOS

One of Dennis Rodman's most inexplicable acts was to kick cameraman Eugene Amos during a game. For no apparent reason, Rodman kicked Amos, who was seated under the basket, in the groin. Rodman was fined $25,000 and suspended for 11 games.

4. HEAD-BUTT OFFICIAL

In a March 16, 1996, game, Rodman was assessed two technical fouls. The Chicago Bulls' forward showed his displeasure by head-butting an official. Rodman was fined $20,000 and given a six-game suspension.

5. HAIR OF A DIFFERENT COLOR

In 1993, after being traded from the Detroit Pistons to the San Antonio Spurs, Dennis Rodman began dyeing his hair different colors. Rodman also stood out with his tattoos, body piercings, and eye makeup.

6. MADONNA

In April 1994, Rodman met pop superstar Madonna during a profile for *Vibe* magazine. It was said to be lust at first sight, but the relationship with Madonna did not last. Rodman gained much of his knack for self-promotion from The Material Girl.

7. CARMEN ELECTRA

In November 1998, Dennis Rodman married actress Carmen Electra in a Las Vegas wedding chapel. Days after the wedding, Rodman filed annulment papers. He then changed his mind, but Electra filed for divorce five months later. And they said it wouldn't last....

8. RODMANTV.COM

In 2000, Rodman came up with something for the fan who could not get enough of him. RODMANTV.com was an Internet site that, for $29.95 per month, a subscriber could visit to check out Dennis's daily activities. Eight cameras were stationed in Rodman's house in the event he was ever at home.

9. RODZILLA

Dennis Rodman seemed a natural for the world of professional wrestling. In 1998, he appeared at a number of wrestling events. Billed as "Rodzilla," he competed in a tag-team match with Hollywood Hogan against Utah Jazz forward Karl Malone and Diamond Dallas Page. Two years later, he headlined *Rodman Down Under,* a pay-per-view wrestling event.

10. PARTY ANIMAL

Dennis Roman likes to party, as his neighbors in Newport Beach, California, found out. Police received 28 complaints from Rodman's neighbors concerning his loud parties. Rodman was no stranger to the police. In December 1999, he was charged with drunk driving, and, a year earlier, a Las Vegas cocktail waitress claimed that he had grabbed her from behind and held her up by her breasts.

Mind Games

Players, coaches, and fans have used mind games to gain a psychological advantage over their opponents.

1. RED AUERBACH

Red Auerbach coached the Boston Celtics to eight consecutive NBA titles. He was notorious for getting into the minds of the opposition. He lit a victory cigar on the bench whenever his team was about to win a game. He frequently baited officials to make sure calls went his way and enjoyed mocking rival fans. Opposing teams claimed he tampered with their dressing rooms and hotels to disrupt their play. Players accused Auerbach of turning off the water in the showers, lowering the heat in the locker rooms, and even setting off fire alarms in hotel rooms to keep them from sleeping. Auerbach also used psychology to motivate his own players. If a player did not perform well, Auerbach might hint that he hoped the player had paid off his mortgage—implying that the player might have seen his last paycheck from the Celtics.

2. LARRY BIRD

Another Boston legend, Larry Bird, enjoyed telling a defender what he was going to do and then doing it. Before a three-point shooting contest, Bird wondered out loud, "I hope you guys are thinking about second place."

3. MICHAEL JORDAN

Michael Jordan was another player who could back up what-ever he said. His ability was so great that he could demoral-ize the opposition. He was not shy about reminding his teammates who was the star. If they did not give him the ball enough or made a mistake, he quickly let them know. He expected teammates to play to his standards. He brought the same intensity to practice that he did to the games. Famed coach Jack Ramsay called him "an assassin in shorts."

4. BILL LAIMBEER

Bill Laimbeer was the center for the championship Detroit Pistons teams of the early 1990s. The baddest of Detroit's "Bad Boys," Laimbeer gained a reputation as a cheap-shot artist. He was a master of throwing opponents off their game through intimidation. Once, he tried to foul a player before the game even started.

5. ADOLPH RUPP

Adolph Rupp won 876 games and lost only 190 during his coaching career at the University of Kentucky from 1931 to 1972. The Baron tried to psych out his opponent even before the game began. During pre-game warm-ups, Rupp ordered his reserves to line up at midcourt and stare at the other team. In 1955, Alabama coach Johnny Dee decided to have his reserves stare back at the Wildcats. Words were exchanged, fisticuffs ensued, and state troopers were called in to break up the brawl. Kentucky won the game 66–52.

6. FRANK McGUIRE

North Carolina coach Frank McGuire felt he needed to do something to disconcert Kansas center Wilt Chamberlain when the Tar Heels met the Jayhawks in the 1957 NCAA title game, so McGuire had 5'7" guard Tommy Kearns jump the opening tip against the 7'1" Chamberlain. Chamberlain was held to 23 points as North Carolina won 54–53 in triple overtime.

7. GARY PAYTON

Guard Gary Payton of the Seattle Super Sonics is one of the NBA's most complete players. An outstanding scorer and superb defender, Payton is also one of the game's most accomplished trash-talkers. He demolishes opponents as much with his words as with his play.

8. BILL RUSSELL

One of the first players to use mind games was Bill Russell. A defensive genius, he intimidated opposing players with his shot-blocking ability. Teammate Tommy Heinsohn called Russell the "foxiest, smartest, meanest player—psychologically—that ever played the game." All-Star Cincinnati Royals' forward Jack Twyman recalled how Russell responded after Twyman had knocked the ball out of his hands a couple of times. Russell elbowed him in the mouth to send a message that Twyman's ball-hawking would not be tolerated.

9. **DAVE BING**

Detroit Pistons' guard Dave Bing had the reputation of being one of basketball's smartest players. The 1967 NBA scoring champion called basketball a "psych game" and tried to gain a mental edge on his opponent. He consistently outsmarted taller defenders, and he believed he could beat an opponent physically if he had the edge mentally.

10. **CAGERS**

In the early days of basketball, the court was frequently enclosed in a cage. One of the reasons for the cage was to protect the players from hostile fans. Even with this protection, fans sometimes injured players by poking them with hat pins, heated nails, and lighted cigarettes.

Home Court Advantage

The basketball spectator is an essential part of any game. Vocal fans have been called a team's sixth player because of their impact on the game. Occasionally, fans get too involved. For instance, at a February 4, 2001, game between the New York Knicks and Miami Heat, singer Jimmy Buffett was ejected by NBA referee Joe Forte for using profanity.

1. SYRACUSE NATIONAL FANS

The Syracuse Nationals of the NBA played in the State Fair Coliseum from 1948 to 1964. The small arena seated just over 4,000 and was a nightmare for opposing teams. The cigarette and cigar smoke was so thick that players had trouble following the flight of the ball. The Syracuse fans did whatever they could to unnerve the opposition. Players inbounding the ball frequently had the hair on their legs pulled out or were jabbed by hat pins. When an opposing player attempted a free throw, fans shook the wires supporting the basket to break the shooter's concentration.

2. **WICHITA FAN**

A Wichita fan thought he'd come up with a sure way to stop the opposition from scoring the winning basket in a 1956 college game against Detroit. With time running out and Wichita leading by one point, a Detroit player took a shot that looked like a game winner. Before the ball arrived, though, a Wichita fan threw his overcoat on top of the basket. The ball hit the coat and bounced away. The referee declared Detroit the winner and ran to the dressing room to avoid being attacked by unhappy fans.

3. **ROBIN FICKER**

One of pro basketball's most rabid and vocal fans was Robin Ficker. Teams dreaded playing the Washington Bullets in the 1980s and having to endure Ficker's verbal barbs. Ficker thoroughly researched each player to find his weakness. No star was immune to Ficker's insults. Chicago's Michael Jordan threw a ball at him, Detroit's Isiah Thomas tried to hit him with a shoe, and Golden State players threw Gatorade on Ficker when they reached their limit of verbal abuse. Boston's Larry Bird called him names, and Philadelphia's Charles Barkley got involved in a shouting match with him. Ficker so angered the Utah Jazz's coach, Frank Layden, that Layden had to be physically restrained from going into the stands after him.

4. **JACK NICHOLSON**

Jack Nicholson is an Academy Award-winning actor best known for his performances in films such as *Easy Rider, Five Easy Pieces, Chinatown,* and *One Flew Over the Cuckoo's Nest.* Nicholson is also one of the most avid fans of the Los Angeles

Lakers. With courtside seats, Nicholson is not shy about making his presence known to opposing players and coaches. In 1980, Dallas coach Dick Motta was trying to give instructions to his team when Nicholson goosed him. Motta wheeled and began punching and kicking him. Only later did he learn that his assailant had been Jack Nicholson. The actor carried on a feud with Boston fans in the 1980s when the Celtics were the Lakers' main rival. In 1984, during the last game of the NBA finals, Nicholson flipped off the fans at the Boston Garden and made other obscene gestures during the Lakers' 111–102 loss. A year later, he allegedly mooned Celtics' fans while standing against the glass of his luxury box.

5. INDIANA PACERS STRIPPERS

Indiana Pacers' fans got an unexpected show from four exotic dancers during a game against the Atlanta Hawks on February 18, 1981. Late in the game, the four topless dancers removed their blouses, revealing their breasts. The well-endowed women brought a halt to the game as players, coaches, and fans turned to the stands to look.

6. CENTRAL MICHIGAN FANS

In 1987, Central Michigan basketball fans started a tradition that got out of hand. To celebrate the first Central Michigan basket of each game, fans threw a roll of toilet paper onto the court. More than 3,000 rolls of tissue came flying from the stands in unison. Players ducked and ran for cover to avoid being struck. The craze resulted in a toilet-paper shortage. The shortage became so acute that toilet paper was being stolen from public restrooms on game day. Finally, a company that made toilet paper agreed to provide free rolls.

In 1988, the tradition came to an end when the Mid-American Conference banned the practice. If any fan tossed toilet paper onto the court, a technical foul was assessed against Central Michigan.

7. TRINITY COLLEGE FANS

Trinity College fans had their own way of celebrating their team's first basket during a February 24, 1954, game against Yale: More than 300 Trinity supporters unleashed chickens from the balcony. Play was stopped in order to round up the birds and clean up the feathers. Yale beat the Bantams 75–66.

8. VANDERBILT FANS

Vanderbilt fans cost their team a game against Florida on January 25, 1989. The Commodores led the Gators 72–70 with time running out when fans began throwing tennis balls at Florida's seven-foot center Dwayne Schintzius. Earlier in the year, Schintzius had been involved in an off-court incident with a tennis racket. Vanderbilt was assessed a technical foul, and Florida tied the game. The prank proved costly, as Florida won 81–78 in overtime.

9. UTAH GAMBLER

During a 1943 NIT game against Kentucky, Utah scored a seemingly meaningless last-second basket, reducing Kentucky's winning margin to eight points. The player was perplexed when a male fan ran onto the court and kissed him. The man was a gambler who'd won a $15,000 bet that Utah would beat the 10-point spread.

10. **SPIKE LEE**

Spike Lee has directed a number of award-winning films, such as *She's Gotta Have It, Do The Right Thing,* and *Malcolm X.* A New York Knicks' fan, Lee frequently got into jawing sessions with Indiana Pacers' star Reggie Miller.

Point Shaving

Bettors use point spreads to bet on basketball games. The point spread attempts to predict the margin of victory. In the 1940s, college basketball players began to accept money from gamblers. Players did not need to lose a game in order to allow gamblers to win their bets against the spread. The point-shaving scandals damaged the reputation of college basketball.

1. CITY COLLEGE OF NEW YORK

College basketball was rocked by a point-shaving scandal in 1951. In January, two Manhattan college players, John Byrnes and Henry Poppe, admitted to fixing three games during the 1949–50 season. They had accepted $1,000 per game from gamblers. By the end of the year, the point-shaving scandals had spread to some of college basketball's most successful teams. Schools that were implicated included City College of New York, Bradley, Kentucky, Long Island University, Manhattan, New York University, and Toledo. Thirty-two players were accused of tampering with the outcomes of at least 86 games played between 1947 and 1950. Long Island University dropped basketball in the wake of the scandal, and famed coach Clair Bee retired. LIU's All-American Sherman White spent eight months in prison for conspiracy to commit bribery and was banned from playing in the NBA. Bradley, runner-up in both the 1950 NIT and NCAA tournaments, had eight players implicated in the scandal. City College of New York, the 1950 NCAA and NIT champion, was devastated by the revelations. Three CCNY players—Ed Roman, Ed Warner, and Al Roth—admitted to accepting $1,500 to shave points. The team, a perennial powerhouse under Coach Nat Holman, never again challenged for a national title.

2. KENTUCKY

When the point-shaving scandal surfaced, Kentucky Coach Adolph Rupp boasted that gamblers could not touch his players with a 10-foot pole. Apparently, the gamblers had longer poles. Three Kentucky players—Ralph Beard, Alex Groza, and Dick Barnstable—admitted to accepting $1,500 to throw a game against Loyola in the 1949 NIT. The fix resulted in a shocking 67–56 defeat. Kentucky then went on to win the NCAA tournament. Beard and Groza, two of college basketball's best players, were banned for life from playing in the NBA.

3. BROOKLYN COLLEGE

Even before the 1951 scandals, college basketball had been tainted by point shaving. In 1945, five members of the Brooklyn College basketball team were arrested in a plot to throw a game against the University of Akron. The players had agreed to accept $1,000 prior to the game plus an additional $2,000 afterwards. When word of the fix got out, the game was cancelled. The players involved were expelled.

4. JACK MOLINAS

Jack Molinas, a rookie on the Fort Wayne Pistons, was banned from the NBA in 1953 for betting on his own team's games while a player at Columbia University. Molinas was averaging more than 12 points a game and had had a promising professional career.

5. JACK EGAN

Ten years after the 1951 point-shaving scandals, another of college basketball's best players was involved in a game-fixing plot. St. Joseph's forward Jack Egan scored 42 points against Utah in the 1961 NCAA consolation game. A third-round draft pick, Egan was not permitted to play in the NBA following revelations that he had been involved in fixing games at St. Joseph's.

6. CHARLIE WILLIAMS

The University of Seattle's leading scorer, Charlie Williams, and teammate Peller Phillips Jr. were arrested in 1965 for their part in fixing a game against Idaho.

7. RICK KUHN

In 1981, Rick Kuhn, a former player at Boston College, was found guilty of shaving points during the 1978–79 season. Kuhn was sentenced to 10 years in prison.

8. TULANE UNIVERSITY

Five Tulane players were accused of shaving points in 1985 games against Memphis State and Southern Mississippi. The players had agreed to shave points in exchange for cash and cocaine. The team's star, John "Hot Rod" Williams, was acquitted, but the program was shut down for five years as a result of the allegations.

9. **STEVEN SMITH**

In 1997, two former Arizona State players, Steve Smith and Isaac Burton Jr., were accused of fixing games during the 1993–94 season. The players received $20,000 per game. Smith had needed the money to pay debts to a bookmaker. The point shaving was uncovered when it was noted that huge bets were being made on Arizona State games.

10. **KENNETH DION LEE**

A year after the Arizona State point-shaving scandal broke, two players at Northwestern faced similar charges. Former Wildcat players Kenneth Dion Lee and Dewey Williams were indicted on shaving points in three games during the 1994–95 season. Lee was paid $4,000 to fix a game against Penn State. The Nittany Lions had been favored by 14 points but won by 30.

Zebras

Basketball officials are known as zebras for their striped shirts. They are not always the most popular men on the court. Bowling Green coach Bob Conibear remarked, "I dreamed I was on safari in Africa and killed every zebra I saw."

1. SID BORGIA

Sid Borgia was one of the NBA's most controversial officials. Borgia worked the league from 1946 to 1966 and was the supervisor of the NBA referees during his last five seasons. Although respected for his ability, he occasionally got involved in fisticuffs with players and fans. During a February 19, 1959, game between the Boston Celtics and Syracuse Nats, Borgia was unmercifully heckled by a fan. A fistfight ensued, and Borgia knocked out several of the abusive spectator's teeth. Later in the game, Borgia was slugged by Boston's Tom Heinsohn when he attempted to break up a fight between Heinsohn and Syracuse's Dolph Schayes. The result was a bench-clearing melee.

2. **STAN STUTZ**

Sid Borgia was also involved in one of the most disputed calls in NBA history. The incident occurred in the opening game of the 1952 NBA championship series between the Minneapolis Lakers and New York Knicks. New York led 13–9 in the first quarter when the Knicks' Al McGuire drove to the basket and was fouled. Neither Sid Borgia nor the other official, Stan Stutz, noticed that McGuire had made the basket, although it seemed that everyone else in the building had seen the ball go in. Instead of being credited with the two-point basket, McGuire made a single free throw. The call proved decisive as the game went into overtime with Minneapolis winning 83–79. The Lakers, with the help of the muffed call, won the series four games to three.

3. **NEW YORK CELTICS**

Decades before the Boston Celtics became one of basketball's most storied franchises, the New York Celtics were a touring professional team. The squad invented a move called the "Celtic Sandwich" to intimidate officials. Two New York players would simultaneously collide with a referee to make sure calls went their way.

4. **CLAYTON TOWNS COUNTY HIGH SCHOOL**

Players from Clayton Towns County High School in Georgia were once so incensed by the officiating in a game that they began shooting at their opponents' basket. They scored 56 points for the other team in a 129–41 defeat.

5. **PAT KENNEDY**

Pat Kennedy, who refereed college games for decades in the New York area, brought showmanship to the art of officiating.

It was impossible for anyone to ignore Kennedy. He screamed out calls, waved his arms, and blew his whistle constantly. His face was beet-red, and the veins bulged in his neck. During a game in the 1930s, Stanford All-American Hank Luisetti, astounded by Kennedy's act, told the ref that he was crazy. During an early professional game between the Boston Visitations and New York Celtics, a player ripped off Kennedy's shirt after being called for a foul. Incredibly, Kennedy finished the game shirtless.

6. JIM DUFFY

On November 6, 1958, referee Jim Duffy threw St. Louis Hawks' center Clyde Lovellette out of an exhibition game in Albuquerque, New Mexico, for arguing a foul call. Lovellette promised to get even with Duffy. Later that night, Lovellette went to Duffy's motel room with a pair of six-shooters loaded with blanks. When Duffy opened the door, Lovellette emptied the guns. Terrified, Duffy ran for cover.

7. KENTUCKY–NEW YORK UNIVERSITY

During the early days of college basketball, officiating often favored the home team; the University of Kentucky, coached by Adolph Rupp, found out the hard way in a 1935 game against New York University played at Madison Square Garden. King Kong Klein and other NYU players repeatedly fouled Kentucky center Leroy "Cowboy" Edwards, but officials refused to blow their whistles. Deprived of numerous free-throw opportunities, Kentucky lost the game 23–22.

8. DON MURPHY

On February 21, 1971, Chicago Bulls' coach Dick Motta protested a call in a game against the Detroit Pistons by drop-kicking the basketball into the balcony. The tantrum should have resulted in a technical foul, but somehow referee Don Murphy did not see the kick. When Detroit coach Butch van Breda Kolff protested, he was given the technical.

9. **FRANK LANE**

Frank Lane is best remembered for being general manager of several major-league baseball teams, including the Chicago White Sox, Cleveland Indians, and St. Louis Cardinals. Before he became a baseball executive, Lane was a college basketball official. He had an embarrassing moment during a February 20, 1932, game between Kentucky and Vanderbilt. Lane called a foul on Vanderbilt's Dutch Kreuter. Kentucky center Aggie Sale was supposed to go to the foul line. Vanderbilt players argued the call, and a flustered Lane inexplicably awarded a foul shot to Vanderbilt. The free throw proved to be the difference as Vanderbilt upset Kentucky 32–31 to end the Wildcats' 15-game winning streak.

10. **JOHN FRASER**

John Fraser refereed nine games in the Missouri Valley Conference during the 1957 season. Large amounts of money were bet on teams that won eight of the nine games. Fraser was relieved of his duties as referee in mid-season. The official reason for the dismissal was a neck injury, but it was widely believed that Fraser was fired for dubious officiating.

Foul Mood

I n a 1953 NBA playoff game between Boston and Syracuse, a record 107 fouls were whistled. Over the years, there have been many players who have been called for more than their share of fouls. In a November 15, 1959, game against the Cincinnati Royals, Syracuse center Connie Dierking fouled out in the first quarter. Steve Johnson led the NBA in disqualifications in 1982, 1986, and 1987. Johnson fouled out of 25 games during the 1981–82 season.

1. VERN MIKKELSON

Vern Mikkelson was the NBA's first great power forward and a major reason that the Minneapolis Lakers dominated the NBA during the 1950s. One record Mikkelson would have preferred not to hold was the mark for most disqualifications in NBA history. Mikkelson fouled out of 127 of the 699 games in which he played. He averaged more than four fouls per game during his career, which lasted from 1949 to 1959.

2. **DON MEINEKE**

Don "Monk" Meineke set a dubious record during his rookie season with the Fort Wayne Pistons in 1953. Meineke fouled out of 26 games and averaged nearly five fouls per game.

3. **DON OTTEN**

Tri-Cities' center Don Otten set a record during a game against Sheboygan that will almost certainly never be broken. Otten was called for eight fouls, the maximum under the existing rules. Today, a player is permitted only six fouls before being disqualified.

4. **RASHEED WALLACE**

Players usually are given technical fouls when they overreact to calls made by officials. Rasheed Wallace of the Portland Trail Blazers has no equal in being assessed technical fouls. During the 1999–00 season, Wallace was called for a record 38 technical fouls. The next season Wallace became the first NBA player to be called for 40 technical fouls.

5. **BOBBY BAILEY**

Bobby Bailey of Newberry College discovered that guarding Furman's Frank Selvy was no easy task. Bailey fouled out in just three minutes of a game played on February 13, 1954. Selvy scored 100 points in a 149–95 victory.

6. **JACK LOOMIS**

Stanford center Jack Loomis fouled out of a January 29, 1972, game against Air Force in just four minutes. He received a standing ovation from the astonished Stanford fans.

7. **DICK FARLEY**

Syracuse's Dick Farley holds the record for the quickest disqualification on fouls in NBA history. In a March 12, 1956, game against St. Louis, Farley fouled out after only five minutes. Despite Farley's foul binge, Syracuse won 97–92.

8. **JOHN CARTY**

University of California's John Carty needed just five minutes to foul out of a February 7, 1988, game against Arizona. He averaged one foul for each minute he played.

9. **JUNGLE JIM LOSCUTOFF**

Jungle Jim Loscutoff was the enforcer on the Boston Celtics. On November 15, 1956, the Boston forward grabbed the shorts of Fort Wayne's George Yardley as he went up for a rebound. The shorts came off, causing Yardley to grab a towel and run to the locker room.

10. **WALTER DUKES**

Walter Dukes of the Detroit Pistons led the NBA in disqualifications for four consecutive years from 1959 to 1962. His 121 disqualifications ranks second in NBA history. During his eight-year pro career, Dukes fouled out in a record 21.8 percent of the games in which he played.

Basketbrawl

Basketball can sometimes be a contact sport. After one of his front teeth was knocked out in a fight with Atlanta's Walt Bellamy, Gus Johnson of the Baltimore Bullets got a false tooth with a gold star imbedded in it.

1. KERMIT WASHINGTON

One of the ugliest incidents in NBA history occurred in a December 1977 game between Houston and Los Angeles. Houston's Rudy Tomjanovich was running to the aid of teammate Kevin Kunnert during a melee when he was sucker-punched by Kermit Washington of the Lakers. Tomjanovich suffered serious injuries to his eye and cheek and missed the remainder of the season. Washington received a 60-day suspension.

2. UNIVERSITY OF MINNESOTA

With 36 seconds remaining in a 1972 game between Ohio State and Minnesota, Buckeye center Luke Witte scored to give his team a 50–44 lead. On the play, Minnesota's Ron Taylor had knocked Witte to the floor. It appeared that Taylor was helping Witte to his feet when he suddenly kneed

Witte in the groin. Taylor's teammate, Ron Behagen, then jumped on Witte's neck and shoulders. Witte and two other Ohio State players were hospitalized as a result of the on-court mugging.

3. LATRELL SPREEWELL

Latrell Spreewell of the Golden State Warriors attacked coach P. J. Carlesimo during a practice session in 1997. The shocking assault resulted in Spreewell being suspended for the remainder of the season. Spreewell was traded to the New York Knicks the next year.

4. INDIANA STATE

Indiana State had several players ejected following a bench-clearing brawl in a 1989 game against Wichita State, and the team was forced to play with only four players. The situation got worse when two more of the Sycamore players fouled out. Not surprisingly, Indiana State lost, 84–69.

5. RED AUERBACH

Boston Celtics' coach Red Auerbach liked to play mind games with the opposition. Prior to a 1957 game against the Hawks in St. Louis, Auerbach complained that the baskets were not even. He became involved in an argument with Hawks' owner Ben Kerner. Auerbach settled the argument by decking Kerner.

6. JOHN CHANEY

Massachusetts defeated Temple 56–55 in a 1994 game. Massachusetts' coach John Calipari was answering questions in a postgame press conference when Temple's coach John Chaney burst into the room and threatened to kill him.

Chaney had to be restrained by University of Massachusetts players. Chaney was given a one-game suspension and later apologized to Calipari for his behavior.

7. **HORACE GRANT**

Seattle's Horace Grant and Chuck Person were injured in a fight during a practice session on March 26, 2000. But they weren't the ones fighting—they were trying to break up a scuffle between teammates Gary Payton and Vernon Maxwell. Grant injured his shoulder during the fight, and Person, who was already on the injured list, aggravated his knee injury.

8. **SOUTH CAROLINA**

South Carolina led Maryland 96–70 with five minutes to play in a 1971 game when the Gamecocks' Rick Aydlett and The Terrapins' Ray Flowers got into a fight under the basket. When Maryland coach Lefty Driesell tried to separate them, he was punched by one of the South Carolina players. Driesell ended up with a swollen lip and a loss as officials suspended play and awarded the victory to South Carolina.

9. **CHARLES OAKLEY**

Everything appeared to be normal on December 1, 2000, when the Los Angeles Clippers completed their morning shoot at Toronto's Air Canada Center in preparation for a game against the Raptors. The Clippers' Jeff McInnis sat down in a courtside seat as the Toronto players took the court. Raptors' forward Charles Oakley held a basketball in his left hand and punched McInnis with his right. Oakley and McInnis had been involved in a dispute over personal matters. Oakley was suspended for three games and fined $15,000.

McInnis, despite swelling on the left side of his face, scored 8 points in a 104–95 loss to the Raptors.

10. **KAREEM ABDUL-JABBAR**

Undeniably one of the greatest players in NBA history, Kareem Abdul-Jabbar was not one of the league's best fighters. During a 1977 fight with Milwaukee Bucks' rookie Kent Benson, Abdul-Jabbar broke his hand. On another occasion, he was decked by Dennis Awtrey.

Incredible Injuries

During a 2000 game, New York Knicks' coach Jeff Van Gundy received a 12-stitch gash when he was accidentally head-butted by Marcus Camby, one of his own players. Throughout the years, basketball players have been injured in a variety of ways.

1. KENYON MARTIN

The University of Cincinnati was ranked number one in the country entering the 2000 Conference USA tournament, but the team's hopes for a national title were compromised when All-American center Kenyon Martin broke his leg in a first-round game against St. Louis. The Bearcats lost the game to the Billikens and, without Martin, were eliminated in the second round of the NCAA tournament by Tulsa. Nevertheless, Martin was later named national player of the year.

2. BOB LANIER

Another injury that cost a team a chance at the national title happened in 1970 to St. Bonaventure center Bob Lanier. He

Kenyon Martin's injury during the 2000 Conference USA tournament was a huge disappointment for University of Cincinnati fans. The Bearcats were ranked number one in the country at the end of the regular season, but the loss of Martin, the national college player of the year, ensured the Bearcats' early departure from the NCAA tournament.

averaged more than 29 points a game during the season, and the Bonnies were considered a threat to win the championship. During a game against Villanova in the East regional finals, Lanier tore the medial collateral ligament in his knee in a collision with the Wildcats' Chris Ford. Without Lanier, St. Bonaventure lost to Jacksonville 91–83 in the national semifinals.

3. **SCOTT MAY**

Indiana's Scott May broke his arm during the 1975 season, and the injury possibly cost the Hoosiers a national title. Indiana was undefeated going into the NCAA tournament. The Hoosiers lost 92–90 to Kentucky in the Mideast regional finals. The next season, with a healthy May, Indiana went undefeated and won the national title.

4. **DENO NICHOLS AND BEN JONES**

Arkansas had qualified to play in the NCAA tournament when disaster struck. Two Razorback players, Deno Nichols and Ben Jones, suffered broken legs when they were struck by a passing car while trying to change a tire. Arkansas withdrew from the tournament and was replaced by Utah. The Utes took advantage of the opportunity and won the tournament.

5. **NYKESHA SALES**

Nykesha Sales of the University of Connecticut appeared certain to break the school scoring record at the end of the 1998 season. She was only one point short of Kelly Bascom's career record of 2,177 points when she ruptured her Achilles tendon. In a strange conclusion to an outstanding career, Sales was inserted into the team's season-ending game even though she was on crutches. She was then permitted to hobble to the basket and score her record-setting points. The points were later stricken from the record books.

6. **MIKE SEWITCH**

Long Island University's Mike Sewitch did not let a broken arm stop him from playing in the 1939 NIT championship game against Loyola of Chicago. Despite his injury, Sewitch held Loyola star Mike Novak to no field goals in a 12-point LIU victory, preserving the team's undefeated season.

7. **LEW ALCINDOR**

Just prior to the 1968 "Game of the Century" matchup against Elvin Hayes and the Houston Cougars, UCLA center Lew Alcindor suffered a scratched left eyeball. With his vision hampered, Alcindor shot only four of 18 from the field as the Bruins were upset by Houston 71–69.

8. **MARVIN BARNES**

Providence and Memphis State met in the 1973 NCAA semifinal game. The Friars led Memphis 24–16 when Providence's Marvin Barnes, one of the nation's best rebounders, dislocated his right kneecap. Barnes returned late in the game, but Providence fell to Memphis State 98–85.

9. **FRANK ANDRESKO**

Possibly the most unusual injury in basketball history occurred in 1929 to Oshkosh player Frank Andresko. He was thrown against the wall and his jersey was torn when the over-inflated basketball that he was dribbling exploded.

10. **RUBEN PATTERSON**

Seattle Super Sonics' forward Ruben Patterson missed a March 24, 2000, game against Utah because of swollen Achilles tendons. He claimed the injury was caused by ill-fitting sneakers.

The Blind Bomber

These players overcame illness and injury to achieve basketball stardom.

1. GEORGE GLAMACK

George Glamack was one of basketball's most remarkable players. He was known as "The Blind Bomber" because his vision was so poor that he could see only a few feet in front of him. He used the lines on the court to judge how hard to shoot. His signature shot was a left-handed hook from the foul line. He holds the distinction of being the first All-American from the University of North Carolina. In 1940, he scored 45 points in a game against Clemson. Glamack averaged more than 20 points per game in 1941. He scored 31 points in the 1941 East regional consolation game against Dartmouth, making him the only player in the first 10 years of the NCAA tournament to score more than 30 points in a game. Twice he was named the Helms Foundation Player of the Year. Despite his poor eyesight, Glamack averaged 9.3 points per game during his professional career.

2. SEAN ELLIOT

Sean Elliot was a two-time All-American at the University of Arizona. He broke Lew Alcindor's Pac-10 Conference record with 2,555 points. In 1989 he won the Wooden Award, given to the college player of the year. As a pro, Elliot averaged 20 points per game for the San Antonio Spurs in 1996 and was a member of the 1999 NBA champion Spurs team. It appeared his career was over when he was diagnosed with a serious kidney ailment. On August 16, 1999, he received a kidney transplant. The organ was donated by his brother. Elliot beat the odds by returning to the San Antonio lineup late in the 2000 season.

3. ALONZO MOURNING

Alonzo Mourning was an All-American at Georgetown and quickly became one of the NBA's premier centers. Between 1992 and 2000, he averaged more than 21 points per game. Mourning was voted the NBA Defensive Player of the Year in 1999 and 2000. Following the 2000 season, the Miami Heat star was diagnosed with focal glomerulosclerosis, the same kidney ailment that sidelined Sean Elliot. Even though he sat out the 2000–01 season because of his illness, Mourning was voted starting center of the Eastern Conference All-Star team by the fans.

4. MAURICE STOKES

The story of Maurice Stokes is one of the most tragic in basketball history. The NBA Rookie of the Year in 1956, Stokes was an All-Star his first three seasons. A tremendous rebounder, he led the NBA one season and once pulled down 38 boards in a game. In March 1958, Stokes hit his head when he fell during a game. A few days later, he collapsed again. Stokes was eventually diagnosed with encephalitis, a crippling brain disease. He lapsed into a coma and was paralyzed for the remainder of his life. His Cincinnati Royals' teammate Jack Twyman became his legal guardian. Stokes died on April 6, 1970, at the age of 36.

5. MAGIC JOHNSON

In 1979, Earvin "Magic" Johnson led Michigan State to the NCAA championship. A three-time NBA MVP, Johnson played on five championship teams with the Lakers between 1980 and 1988. He announced his retirement in 1991 when he revealed that he was HIV-positive. Johnson came out of retirement in 1996 and showed that he could still play by averaging 14.6 points per game.

6. TOMMY BOYER

Tommy Boyer starred for the University of Arkansas despite having only one eye. An outstanding foul shooter, Boyer twice led the nation twice in free-throw percentage. Boyer made 125 of 134 free throws during the 1961–62 season for a .933 percentage.

7. DAVE BING

When he was five years old, Dave Bing fell on a nail while playing. The nail pierced his left eye, forever blurring his vision. Despite his handicap, Bing became an All-American at Syracuse and in 1967 was the NBA Rookie of the Year with the Detroit Pistons. Midway through his professional career, Bing suffered a partially detached retina when he was poked in his right eye. He returned to play in the NBA despite having serious injuries in both eyes.

8. BENNIE FULLER

Bennie Fuller averaged 44.9 points per game for the Arkansas School for the Deaf during the 1971–72 season. The next year, the hearing-impaired player averaged 50.9 points.

9. WILEY BROWN

Wiley Brown played forward for the Louisville Cardinals despite having an artificial right thumb. Brown forgot to bring his thumb to the arena the night Louisville was to play UCLA in the 1980 NCAA championship game. The team manager rushed to the hotel and found the thumb in a trash bin. With his thumb attached, Brown scored eight points as Louisville defeated UCLA 59–54 for the national championship. In 1978, Brown and teammates Derek Smith and Daryle Cleveland invented the high-five congratulatory hand slap.

10. JIM POLLARD

Jim Pollard was Stanford's leading scorer during the 1942 season, averaging 16 points per game. Pollard came down with the flu prior to the 1942 NCAA title game against Dartmouth. Without their star player, Stanford still managed to defeat Dartmouth 53–38.

Death in the Afternoon

In 1927, 10 members of the Baylor basketball team were killed when their bus was hit by a train during a torrential rainstorm near Austin, Texas. Since that time, many college basketball players have passed away during their prime.

1. HANK GATHERS

Hank Gathers led the nation in both scoring and rebounding while playing for Loyola Marymount in 1989. On March 4, 1990, Loyola Marymount played Portland in the semifinal game of the West Coast Conference tournament. In front of a horrified crowd, Gathers collapsed on the court and died two hours later. It was determined that the cause of Gathers's death was a heart ailment.

2. WAYNE ESTES

Utah State's Wayne Estes was one of college basketball's most prolific scorers of the 1960s. During the 1964–65 season, Estes averaged 33.7 points, second in the country behind Miami's Rick Barry and ahead of Princeton's Bill Bradley. On February 8, 1965, he scored 48 points in a game against Denver. On the way home, Estes stopped at the site of an automobile accident. He was killed instantly when his head brushed against a downed power line. Estes became the first player to be posthumously named to the All-American team.

3. LEN BIAS

The Boston Celtics believed that they had their next great player when they selected University of Maryland All-American Len Bias with the second pick of the 1986 draft. Tragically, Bias died of a cocaine overdose two days later.

4. REGGIE LEWIS

Reggie Lewis was an All-Star guard with the Boston Celtics. On April 29, 1993, he collapsed in a playoff game against Charlotte. Lewis was examined and received conflicting opinions on whether he could continue his basketball career. Three months later, on July 27, Lewis collapsed and died while shooting baskets at Brandeis University. His death was attributed to an enlarged heart.

5. PETE MARAVICH

The greatest scorer in college basketball history, Pete Maravich was also an NBA scoring champion. He retired in 1980 with an NBA career scoring average of 24.2. On January 5, 1988, Maravich died of a heart attack following a game of basketball. Pistol Pete was only 40 years old.

6. BOBBY PHILLS

Bobby Phills averaged 11 points per game during his NBA career with the Cleveland Cavaliers and Charlotte Hornets from 1991 to 2000. The 30-year-old Phills was killed on January 12, 2000, in an automobile accident. He had lost control of his Porsche while racing teammate David Wesley.

7. **MALIK SEALY**

Four months after Bobby Phills's death, another NBA veteran was killed in an automobile accident. Malik Sealy played for the Indiana Pacers, Los Angeles Clippers, Detroit Pistons, and Minnesota Timberwolves from 1992 to 2000. Sealy was returning home from teammate Kevin Garnett's twenty-fourth birthday party when he was killed in a head-on crash. Like Phills, Sealy was 30 years old.

8. **ALTON CROOK**

Alton Crook suffered one of the most mysterious deaths in college basketball history. The West Texas State University freshman walked to a gas station with a five-gallon can. A few moments after he filled the can, he returned in flames and collapsed at the feet of the attendant.

9. **CHRIS STREET**

Iowa forward Chris Street averaged 14 points per game and was the team's leading rebounder during the 1992 season. On January 19, 1993, Street attended a team dinner. On the way home, he was killed instantly when his car collided with a snowplow.

10. **HARRY KERSENBROCK**

Coach Phog Allen was excited when Harry Kersenbrock enrolled at Kansas in 1928. One of the game's first seven-footers, Kersenbrock was expected to be a dominant player. His promising career ended before it even began when he was drowned in a boating accident prior to his first game at Kansas.

Buzzer Beaters

Last-second game-winning shots have provided basketball with some of its most exciting moments. In a 1981 NCAA East regional game, Brigham Young guard Danny Ainge drove the length of the court and made a lay-up to beat Notre Dame at the buzzer. Fourteen years later, UCLA's Tyus Edney duplicated Ainge's feat in the West regional to defeat Missouri. Perhaps the game's best buzzer beater was Vanderbilt's Barry Goheen. Six times during the 1988–89 season, Goheen won games with last-second baskets. Let's close the book with some of basketball's most memorable buzzer beaters.

1. LES HENSON

Virginia Tech and Florida State were tied 77–77 with time running out in a 1980 game played at Tallahassee. Les Henson threw in a length-of-the-court shot at the buzzer to give Virginia Tech a thrilling victory. The shot was measured at 89 feet.

2. MILES SIMON

With time running out in a 1996 game against Cincinnati, Arizona's Miles Simon threw up a desperation 65-foot shot. The ball banked off the backboard for the winning three-pointer as the Wildcats stunned the Bearcats 79–76.

3. ERNIE CALVERLEY

Rhode Island's Ernie Calverley made one of the most memorable shots in NIT history during the first round of the 1946 tournament. His 58-foot shot at the buzzer spelled defeat for Bowling Green.

4. U. S. REED

Arkansas met defending national champion Louisville in the 1981 Midwest regional. The Razorbacks' U. S. Reed made a 50-footer with time running out to defeat Louisville 74–73.

5. BOBBY STEVENS

One of the most dramatic shots in NIT history occurred in the 1973 championship game. Virginia Tech's Bobby Stevens sank a 75-footer in the closing seconds of overtime to defeat Notre Dame 92–91.

6. HERB WILKINSON

Utah and Dartmouth went into overtime in the 1944 NCAA championship game. Freshman Herb Wilkinson made a shot from beyond the top of the key with three seconds remaining to give Utah a 42–40 victory.

7. **BRYCE DREW**

Valparaiso used the old hook-and-ladder play to defeat Mississippi in the first round of the 1998 NCAA Midwest regional. Bill Jenkins passed the ball to Bryce Drew, who sank a three-pointer at the buzzer for a 70–69 win.

8. **JERROD WEST**

Thanks to Jerry West, the Mountaineers' greatest player, West is a revered name in West Virginia University basketball. In the second round of the 1998 NCAA West regionals, another West, Jerrod, banked a three-pointer to give the Mountaineers a 75–74 victory over Cincinnati.

9. **ROLANDO BLACKMAN**

Top-ranked Oregon State played Kansas State in the second round of the 1981 NCAA West regionals. Kansas State's Rolando Blackman hit a 17-footer from the right baseline at the buzzer to give his team a 50–48 win.

10. **JAY ROBERTS**

Kansas and Kansas State played a memorable championship game in the 1962 Big Eight holiday tournament. Kansas' Jay Roberts made a turnaround jumper at the buzzer to defeat Kansas State 90–88 in four overtimes.

Bibliography

Bjarkman, Peter. *The Biographical History of Basketball.* Chicago: Masters Press, 2000.

Clark, Patrick. *Sports Firsts.* New York: Facts on File, 1981.

Douchant, Mike. *Encyclopedia of College Basketball.* Detroit: Visible Ink, 1995.

Fischler, Stan and Shirley. *The Best, Worst and Most Unusual in Sports.* New York: Fawcett Crest, 1977.

Gould, Todd. *Pioneers of the Hardwood.* Bloomington: Indiana University Press, 1998.

Hill, Bob and Randall Bacon. *The Amazing Basketball Book.* Louisville: Devyn Press, 1988.

Hollander, Zander and Alex Sachare. *The Official NBA Encyclopedia.* New York: Villard, 1989.

Kerkhoff, Blair. *The Greatest Book of College Basketball.* Lenexa: Addax Publishing, 1998.

Mendell, Ronald. *Who's Who in Basketball.* New Rochelle: Arlington House, 1973.

Nash, Bruce and Allan Zullo. *The Basketball Hall of Shame.* New York: Pocket Books, 1991.

Pepe, Phil and Zander Hollander. *The Book of Sports Lists.* Los Angeles: Pinnacle, 1979.

Phillips, Louis and Burnham Holmes. *The Complete Book of Sports Nicknames.* Los Angeles: Renaissance Books, 1998.

Sachare, Alex. *The 100 Greatest Basketball Players of All Time.* New York: Pocket Books, 1997.

Wallechinsky, David. *The Complete Book of the Olympics.* New York: Penguin, 1988.

Walton, David and John Hareas. *The Sporting News 2000–2001 Official NBA Register.* St. Louis: Sporting News, 2000.

Yee, Min. *The Sports Book.* New York: Holt, Rinehart and Winston, 1975.

Index

About the Author

Floyd Conner is a lifelong fan of basketball and the author of eleven books. His sports books include *Baseball's Most Wanted, Football's Most Wanted, Golf's Most Wanted, Day By Day in Cincinnati Bengals History,* and *This Date in Sports History.* He also co-authored *Day By Day in Cincinnati Reds History* and the best-selling *365 Sports Facts a Year Calendar.* He lives in Cincinnati with his wife, Susan, and son, Travis.